What's the Smoke For?

*And Other Burning Questions
about the Liturgy*

Johan van Parys

LITURGICAL PRESS
Collegeville, Minnesota

www.litpress.org

1	2	3	4	5	6	7	8	9

Library of Congress Cataloging-in-Publication Data

Van Parys, Johan.
    What's the smoke for? : and other burning questions about the liturgy / Johan van Parys.
        pages   cm
    ISBN 978-0-8146-3565-0 — ISBN 978-0-8146-3590-2
    1. Catholic Church—Liturgy—Miscellanea.   2. Catholic Church—Customs and practices—Miscellanea.   3. Worship—Miscellanea.
    I. Title.

BX1970.V319   2014
264'.02—dc23   2014009365

Contents

Introduction

A long time ago I became aware of an interesting Buddhist story. I have used it many times, taking the liberty to translate it into a Catholic context. My version of the story is set in the fourteenth century in a French abbey. Jehan, who grew up on a nearby farm, recently entered the abbey. He was very happy but missed his cat. One day, while on a walk, he fortuitously ran into his beloved cat. Jehan quickly hid the cat under his habit and made his way back to the abbey. As fate will have it, he ran into the abbot. Noticing that something was awry, the abbot asked him about his whereabouts. Jehan was so nervous that he squeezed the cat too tightly and, in pain, the cat meowed. Having been exposed, the novice fell to his knees, begged for forgiveness, and brazenly asked for permission to keep the cat. To his surprise, the abbot agreed on the condition that the cat not interfere with their monastic life. All was well until one day the cat walked into the church during evening prayer and jumped on the abbot's lap. Annoyed by the incident, the abbot ordered Jehan to tie up the cat before evening prayer. Dutifully, the young monk found the cat every day and tied it up so the monks would not be disturbed during evening prayer. Even after the election of a new abbot, Jehan, now a full-fledged monk, continued to tie up the cat before evening prayer began. On the day the cat passed away, the new abbot promptly sent Jehan to the market to buy a new cat so he could tie it up in order for evening prayer to begin.

Many of us have grown up immersed in our Catholic traditions. Often we don't know why we do what we do, yet we keep on doing it. It is good to occasionally pause and ponder a question or two so we don't end up mindlessly buying a cat so we can tie it up in order for evening prayer to begin.

What's the Smoke For? intends to offer you just that, the opportunity to ponder ninety-one questions pertaining to the liturgy. The inspiration for this book is the *Ask Johan* column that has been part of *Basilica*, the magazine of the Basilica of Saint Mary in Minneapolis, since 1998.

That year I was asked by Margaret Nelson, one of the founding editors of *Basilica*, to write a recurring column. She intended it to be a question-and-answer column. The questions she imagined would come from parishioners. The answers she envisioned to be in a tone reminiscent of both Miss Manners and Bishop Fulton Sheen. She wanted a good theological foundation, accessible language, and the occasional twist so people would actually want to read it. Today *Ask Johan* is still part of *Basilica* and is one of its most popular pages.

When I read through the columns in preparation for this book, I noticed that some questions/answers were too Basilica specific. Others had not yet been answered, while some I answered more than once. Just so you know, the most frequently posed question was about incense. Thus, though based on *Ask Johan* and written in the same style, *What's the Smoke For?* is much more than just a compilation of those columns. This book contains questions/answers solicited from a great variety of people, including new and longtime Catholics alike. In the interest of full disclosure I may have inserted an occasional question myself only because I believe it should have been asked.

May I suggest you have a quick read and then keep this book handy? Maybe you can keep it on your desk, in your glove compartment, or even in your purse. You never know when someone will ask you why the monks tie up a cat so evening prayer can begin.

Liturgical Art
and Architecture

Dear Johan,

After Midnight Mass, my daughter asked me what the smoke was all about. Though I know incense is a very Catholic thing, I was unable to answer her question. Can you help me?

Gentle Reader—

First off, it's not just a Catholic thing, it is also an Orthodox thing, and even more so. But, thank you for asking as this seems to be a burning question for many.

Not too long ago I gave a talk on the sensory aspects of the liturgy. Naturally, I sang the praises of the olfactory sense and lauded the use of incense. No sooner was I done than a person sitting in the front row jumped up. Speaking louder than was necessary, she yelled out: "When will the Catholic Church stop smoking?" Then she grabbed her bag and stomped out. I was speechless.

It seems like people either really love incense or absolutely hate it. Very few people are opinion-less when it comes to incense. Admittedly, some individuals are incense-intolerant due to allergies or respiratory conditions. We need to be very considerate of this.

The use of incense is an important element in Catholic liturgy because of historical, theological, and liturgical reasons.

- Historically, we can trace our use of incense back to Jewish religious rites as well as Roman imperial ceremonies.
- Theologically, the use of incense is connected with Psalm 141, which compares our prayers rising up to God with the rising incense used during our prayers: "My prayers rise like incense."

• Liturgically, incense is used as an honorific gesture. In addition, incense is used because of its olfactory qualities.

In recent times we have become more aware of the importance of the senses. Remember, for example, how the slightest whiff of a certain perfume can whisk you off to a totally different place and time, as it reminds you of a certain person or event. Similarly, incense is used as a reminder of the sacred so that every time we smell it we are reminded that we are at prayer. Taking it a step further, some churches use a different kind of incense for each season of the liturgical year, so as to create an olfactory connection between a liturgical season and a liturgical scent. As soon as people smell a certain aroma, they are transported into a certain liturgical season. Thus, liturgical colors, liturgical music, liturgical texts, and liturgical scent mark the liturgical seasons.

Many churches have abandoned the use of incense out of consideration for people who are physically intolerant of it. This is especially the case in smaller churches where there is little or no airflow. Though this is, of course, very important in terms of creating a hospitable liturgical environment, it also results in the loss of an ancient visual and olfactory symbol. Some parishes have worked to improve their airflow systems so they can continue to use incense without irritating some parishioners. Other parishes have declared certain liturgies incense free while retaining the custom in others. Whatever we do, we need to be sensitive both to the comfort of our parishioners as well as to the important legacy of our symbols.

May I ask you, did your daughter love it or hate it? It may give us an insight into the liturgical future of the use of incense.

Dear Johan,

I saw a young woman with crosses as earrings and at least a dozen rosaries and several pectoral crosses around her neck. I was appalled. It seems to me that the cross is the most important symbol of Christianity. How dare she mock it so?

Gentle Reader—

I must have seen the same woman recently, or else this has become an unhappy trend.

Your question reminds me of a scene that played out many years ago. My younger brother came home from university with a small silver crucifix dangling from his ear. Without saying a word, my mom walked over to him and took it (read: yanked it) out of his ear. To this day I am not sure what displeased my mom the most: the fact that he had his ear pierced or the fact that he wore a cross as an earring.

The cross is the most recognizable symbol of Christianity. However, as is the case with many things we now take for granted, it has not always been thus. It took a while before the cross and especially the crucifix or any other depictions of Christ, Mary, and the saints were accepted. Two factors were at play.

First, early Christians displayed a general timidity toward imagery at best and engaged in the occasional full-fledged period of iconoclasm at worst. It was not until the Second Council of Nicea (787) that matters were settled once and for all. After tumultuous debates, this council not only denounced iconoclasm but it also called for the depictions of Christ, Mary, and the saints with the admonition that when one adores an image one really adores the one represented by the image.

Second, the death of Jesus on the cross was neither expected by his followers nor was it readily embraced. Death by crucifixion was one of the worst condemnations. Roman citizens, for example, could not be punished by crucifixion. In a sense, the cross was experienced as a scandal and an embarrassment. So they concentrated on the resurrection, rather than on the death of Jesus.

Gradually the Christian community came to embrace the scandal of the cross as the mystery of salvation. And by the early third century the cross had become closely associated with Christianity. Clement of Alexandria (150–ca. 215) referred to the cross as τὸ κυριακὸν σημεῖον or the Lord's sign. And according to Tertullian (160–220) Christians are *crucis religiosi* or devotees of the cross.

Today the cross is ubiquitous and it is undoubtedly the most recognizable symbol in the entire world. We top our church steeples with crosses. We hang crosses in our homes, in our cars, and around our necks. We even tattoo crosses on our bodies. Most often this is done in good faith and in good taste. Sometimes it is done in a misguided attempt at unfortunate fashion. In some rare and regrettable instances the cross is intentionally desecrated.

Although I can understand why the sight of the young woman may have given you cause for concern, let's take consolation in the fact that by the cross we have been saved and nothing can take that away, not even ill-advised use or malicious abuse.

Dear Johan,

I find some depictions of Jesus on the cross rather disturbing. I can't remember the name of the German artist but his crucifixion was just terrifying. Wouldn't it suffice to just have a cross?

Gentle Reader–

For starters, let's agree that a cross does not have a corpus or depiction of Jesus on it, while a crucifix does. Most Protestant churches exclusively prefer the use of a cross while the Catholic church favors the crucifix.

The crucifix you are referring to must be one by Matthias Grünewald (ca. 1470–1528). His crucifixion scenes are indeed rather gruesome and difficult to behold. However, they do make a point.

Like you, Christians have struggled with the depiction of Jesus on the cross from the very beginning. As a result they were very hesitant to use what later became the most recognizable Christian symbol of them all. Instead they used Christ monograms, anchors, a fish, a shepherd. When they timidly started using the cross it was without the corpus. Most often a victory wreath decorated the cross. Though early Christians recognized Jesus' sacrifice on the cross as the portal to salvation, they were hesitant to represent Jesus on the cross.

Starting in the fourth century Christians began slowly to represent Jesus on the cross. However, when they did they depicted Jesus as completely in charge. It is as if he is standing on the cross using a wooden footstool that is attached to the cross. Both hands and both feet are nailed to the cross. His eyes are wide open and he looks directly at the beholder.

The next step was the representation of the suffering Jesus on the cross. Rather than standing on the cross, Jesus hangs from the cross. His feet are placed on one another and one nail is used for both feet. His body shows signs of torture. He often wears the crown of thorns as described in the gospels. This type of crucifix appears during the time of state decline after the fall of the Roman and Carolingian empires. Europe sank into the so-called dark ages, which were characterized by political anarchy, war and violence, famine, and diseases such as the plague that decimated more than half the population. The people's feelings of despair and suffering are clearly reflected in the way they depicted Christ. In a sense they depicted their own suffering on the cross or they took consolation in connecting their suffering to that of Jesus.

The Renaissance with its interest in realism keeps depicting the suffering Christ but with less of the exaggerated gore so typical for many of the medieval depictions. Although Christ is still shown as dying on the cross, there is a quality of stillness surrounding the cross. Although there is realism in the depiction, there is also rational restraint.

The Baroque renditions, which are part of the Counter-Reformation efforts of the Catholic Church, are all about the drama of the moment as they show Longinus, one of the Roman soldiers, piercing the side of Jesus. Mary, the mother of Jesus, faints into the arms of John, the beloved, and Mary of Magdala embraces the foot of the cross. The sacrifice of the cross is greatly emphasized in these depictions in support of the theology of the sacrifice of the Mass, which is often celebrated beneath them.

The late eighteenth and nineteenth centuries, which are characterized by a return to earlier artistic styles, embrace the medieval depiction in the Romanesque and Gothic style but these neo-versions lack the character of the images they imitate. Rather there is a romantic softness and a form of spiritualization in the crucifixes that are typical for the piety of this period.

The twentieth and twenty-first centuries have all of the above and much more. Though there was a clear trend in the Catholic Church to move away from the crucifix in favor of a cross or a risen Christ on a cross, new directives indicate that a crucifix needs to be placed in each sanctuary and processional crosses need to actually be processional crucifixes.

This is probably more than you asked for. I could have answered with a simple no but what good would that have done?

Dear Johan,

I received a plastic glow-in-the-dark statue of the Blessed Virgin as a gift. I am not sure what to think of it. Is this sacred art? Or can I toss it?

Gentle Reader—

When in doubt never make the mistake to toss what purports to be art, especially sacred art. You did well to ask before making an irrevocable mistake. After you read my answer, you may be better equipped to make the decision, or not.

"Is this sacred art?" is a question that is often posed and pondered. Twenty years ago I would have answered "no" without any hesitation and would have counseled you to dispose of it *quam primum*, with haste. In addition, I would have happily slipped you a catalogue of other artistic travesties to avoid.

Living in the proverbial ivory tower, I was convinced that only "high art" could be considered sacred art. The occasional accusation of elitism had little impact on my thinking. Surely, no one could ever deny that such world-famous art as the frescoes in the Sistine Chapel are sacred art of the highest quality? And who was audacious enough to erroneously suggest that glow-in-the-dark statues of Mary were sacred art? The lines between good and bad sacred art were clear to me and they needed to be drawn and defended.

My thinking started to change when I was gifted a somewhat unusual representation of Our Lady of Guadalupe. Intrigued but not impressed, I placed it with the other religious kitsch I received over the years. And yet, every time I walked by it, I was drawn to it. The image kept beckoning me until I gave in and considered it more closely. To the surprise of many, it ended up in an exhibit about Mary. When a friend saw it there, he admitted that he had always thought of this particular image as just one of my religious *tchotchkes*. Seeing it under glass and in good lighting, he finally realized it was sacred art. And so did I.

Thanks to Our Lady of Guadalupe and all she stands for, I became less rigorous and more forgiving when it comes to sacred art. Nevertheless, not everything goes. I still hold that there indeed is such a thing as bad sacred art. Is this a contradiction in terms?

When considering sacred art allow me to suggest three qualities.

First, sacred art needs to be authentic art. This requires an authentic esthetic as well as the use of authentic materials. In the past I thought certain esthetics or styles superior to others. Today I realize that the church is quite correct when upholding that there is no superior style, but that each period and region necessarily provides its own form of authentic art in response to the needs of each specific time and place.

Second, sacred art needs to have a sacred message. This is easily accomplished in figurative art that depicts the life of Jesus, Mary, or the saints. But what about abstract art that deals with such religious notions as light and darkness or life and death? Can this be considered sacred art? Since certain abstract art forces us to deal with deeply religious matters like life and death, it truly has a sacred message, though this may not be obvious to everyone, at least not at first.

Third, sacred art needs to be able to communicate its sacred message. In other words, people need to be able to be inspired by sacred art and receive its sacred message. What makes this aspect of sacred art difficult to grasp is that all of us have different intellectual interests and spiritual sensibilities. As a result we are moved by different kinds of art. Some people may be deeply inspired by a poor print of bad religious art while they are supremely untouched by a celebrated example of sacred art. Other people may find abstract art intensely spiritual while a graphic depiction of the martyrdom of an obscure saint, though by definition sacred, does nothing for them. This reality ought to make us more generous when considering sacred art because the fact that one person is spiritually moved by an image does not necessarily make it sacred art. At the same time, the fact that a person is not moved by a certain image does not necessarily make it bad sacred art, either. In both cases, the beholder should not absolutize his or her personal experience of the art.

So, what to do with your glow-in-the-dark Mary or any other questionable religious art you may harbor in your home? Please consider the three above-mentioned qualities of sacred art. Should you find your art lacking I suggest you do one of two things. Either you store it with your beloved yet secret velvet image of Elvis Presley. Or you send it to me and who knows, one day it may appear in an exhibit. And as my friend helped me discover, when placed in a glass vitrine under beautiful lighting, what was once thought a mere *tchotchke* may turn out to be fine art.

Dear Johan,

Would you please settle an argument I am having with my wife: did St. Francis invent the nativity scene or did he not?

Gentle Reader—

I am all for settling arguments, especially between spouses. I cannot but wonder who will come out on the winning end.

Saint Francis is often credited with the initiation of such popular devotions as the Stations of the Cross and the nativity scene. Though it is true that this medieval saint and his enthusiastic followers popularized these devotions, he did not really invent them.

Among some of the oldest depictions of the nativity are a third-century fresco in the Roman catacomb of Priscilla and a fourth-century stone carving on a Roman sarcophagus now housed in a church in Milan. Since those early depictions, the nativity has been ubiquitously frescoed onto church walls, carved into cathedral portals, and painted in prayer books.

The novelty of the nativity scene organized by St. Francis was that it was a living nativity scene and thus it was three-dimensional. According to his biographer, St. Bonaventure, Francis staged his first live nativity scene in the town of Greccio, Italy, in 1223.

Francis's special devotion to the nativity scene had two basic reasons. On the one hand, he was inspired by a trip to the Holy Land, when he realized that one did not have to be there to celebrate the important moments in the life of Jesus. With the help of art one could do that fruitfully anywhere in the world. On the other hand, his devotion was encouraged by his disappointment with the celebration of Christmas in his homeland. Using the nativity scene, he wanted to refocus his contemporaries' attention on the reason for the celebration of Christmas. Doesn't that sound like a familiar problem?

Having received the papal blessing, the custom of live nativities spread with the Franciscans throughout the continent. Elaborate reenactments of the story of the nativity developed as a great teaching tool, especially for the illiterate masses. As with many good things, these well-intentioned reenactments quickly started overshadowing the celebration of Christmas. As a result, they were abolished and the live scenes were replaced with statues. These gradually made their way from church yards and portals into our homes.

So, let's say you are both correct. Though Francis did not invent the nativity scene, he was very important in its popularization.

Dear Johan,

I was told that Pope Emeritus Benedict XVI does not believe that there was an ox and a donkey present in the stable where Jesus was born. And by the way, is it a crèche or a manger? I get confused.

Gentle Reader—

Let me start with the part of the question that does not relate to papal pronouncements: crèche or manger? *Crèche* is an Old French word that is derived from the Old High German *krippa*, meaning crib. The word manger, from the Old English *mangeour*, is derived from the Old French *maingeure*, to eat, which, in turn, is derived from the Latin *manducare*, to chew. So, though both words relate to the place where Jesus was laid, the one calls it a baby's crib, the other a feeding trough. The latter, of course, is more in line with the Scriptures: "[A]nd she gave birth to her firstborn son. She wrapped him in swaddling clothes and laid him in a manger, because there was no room for them in the inn" (Luke 2:7).

With regard to the presence or absence of a donkey and ox, allow me to say that since the earliest depictions of the nativity artists have always reflected the theology of the time, their own spirituality, and even their day-to-day experiences in their art. One of the earliest depictions of the nativity we know is found on a fourth-century Roman sarcophagus currently preserved in Milan. It simply shows the baby Jesus wrapped in swaddling clothes, laying in a manger with a donkey on one side and an ox on the other. The beholder is to fill in the rest of the story.

Though neither animal is mentioned in the gospels, artists may have presumed that if Jesus was born in a stable, animals would have been present. Another, more deeply theological, explanation is a reference found in the book of the prophet Isaiah: "An ox knows its owner, / and an ass, its master's manger; / But Israel does not know, / my people has not understood" (Isa 1:3). Thus the presence of an ox and donkey is an affirmation of the fact that

Jesus is indeed the Messiah. Since written documents that link the depiction of the ox and donkey to this biblical passage postdate the first depictions, it may or may not have influenced the artists. Nevertheless, to us it provides a deeper level of meaning to the presence of these animals in the stable.

On an aside, I just found a wonderful nativity scene from the Amazon region of Brazil. In this rendition the artist replaced the traditional ox and donkey with some kind of wild boars. I am pretty sure there were no wild boars present at the birth of Jesus and I am pretty sure you will find no biblical substantiation for them either, and yet they are there. Who knows, maybe a few centuries from now someone will be writing about the historical and theological meaning of wild boars in the nativity scene.

Dear Johan,

I suspect our new pastor has gone mad. He was given some sort of primitive-looking colorful wood carving by his previous parishioners and now he insists on installing it in our beautiful Gothic church. It would ruin the artistic integrity of our building. I am beside myself. What should I do?

Gentle Reader—

Deep cleansing breaths: in with the art, out with the bad. And again . . .

It sounds like your pastor is attached to the art and does not care a bit about stylistic purity. So I suggest you learn to love it because I don't suspect it will go away anytime soon. Maybe I can assist you in this process by simply easing your obsession with stylistic purity. The best thing for you to do would be to take a trip to Europe to visit the many, many cathedrals, churches, and chapels that would not pass your purity test. I am quite sure you will love them nonetheless. But short of such a trip, just a few words.

Let me begin by assuring you that you are not the only person who thinks that buildings, especially church buildings, should be stylistically pure. Even some well-educated people surprisingly subscribe to this theory. According to them, the highest form of church architecture is a church that has been built in one specific style and retains this purity of style throughout the ages. And, of course, this style is preferably Romanesque, Gothic, Baroque, or one of their neo-renditions. For people who belong to this school of thinking, to have contemporary art in a beaux-arts building, for example, would be considered a great artistic and even a theological blunder. No disrespect intended, I suspect it is somewhat of a young countries' syndrome.

Just one lesson in the history of ecclesiastical architecture would, of course, be enough to debunk these kinds of thought. Suffice it to look at the great European cathedrals. They proudly and very effectively bear the imprint of each generation that has worked on them and worshiped in them. Romanesque naves, Gothic apses, Baroque altars, and contemporary appointments create a wonderful testimony to the faith of the many, many generations who have gone before us. And like the church in her great diversity is one, these buildings in their stylistic richness are supremely harmonious.

As to the mental condition of your pastor, I would hesitate to declare him mad on account of his choice to bring contemporary art into your Gothic, presumably neo-Gothic, building. That seems a bit extreme and given my answer you may already have declared me likewise.

One more thing, maybe he can take you on that much needed trip to Europe?

Dear Johan,

I hate contemporary abstract art. I don't understand it. It's ugly. It has no spiritual meaning. It has no place in the church. Why do some people insist on forcing contemporary art on us? We don't need it. We don't want it.

Gentle Reader—

No need to get so excited. It sure is not good for your health. Let us consider a couple of things together.

For starters, it is a great consolation to me, as it should be to you, that even Michelangelo, who was undeniably one of the greatest artists of all times, was a contemporary artist at one point who was revered by some and reviled by others.

The same holds for many artists who are widely loved and admired today. Take, for example, French composer Maurice Ravel (1875–1937). When dedicating a newly composed string quartet to his teacher Gabriel Fauré (1845–1924), Fauré told him that this was very kind but he could not accept since the piece was ugly, had no meaning, and was completely unintelligible. Publicly humiliated, Ravel doubted his talents and almost stopped composing. Thankfully, fellow composer Claude Debussy (1862–1918), who loved Ravel's work, encouraged him to continue writing music. String Quartet in F is now one of the most celebrated works in French string music and Ravel is known and loved throughout the world.

The appreciation of art is often very subjective and our subjective appreciation depends mostly on the taste of the community we live in. Very few people venture beyond this comfort zone. By contrast, great artists, the kind of artists who will be remembered almost by definition, venture beyond this comfort zone as they have the gift of seeing what most of us cannot see, except when these artists allow us a peek into the world they see through their art.

Sometimes their vision is complex. Often their art is unusual and maybe uncomfortable. However, it is not because we don't "like it" that it is bad art. It may take more effort on our part to appreciate and understand contemporary art, but just remember that the artists we all love and appreciate were "modern" artists at one point and they too were scorned for their "modern" art, even by other artists.

With regard to your distaste for abstract art I am afraid there is little I can do as you seem quite convinced. But just in case, I ask you to consider this one premise: figurative art imposes imagery while abstract art invites imagery.

Figurative art, of course, has served us well in the telling of our Christian story. There is, however, one danger in that figurative art runs the risk of imposing imagery. This fact can easily be illustrated by asking a group of people about certain biblical scenes. They visualize them just as they have seen them in the pictures, regardless whether these pictures were historically accurate or not. Take, for example, the conversion of St. Paul. The most popular depictions of this important moment in his life show him falling off his horse. When asked, that is what people will tell you happened despite the fact that the Scriptures do not mention a horse at all. The image is imprinted on people's minds, even those who are familiar with the Scriptures. This is an innocent example, but what about Mary and Jesus being depicted with blond hair and blue eyes? What does that image do to our religious imagination?

By contrast, abstract art does not impose images; rather abstract art invites imagination. That makes it less obvious and less utilized as an evangelization tool as it demands more work on the part of the viewer. Yet, despite this, it enjoys the capacity for a deeper and more genuine reception of the Bible message.

Did I convince you? I doubt I did. At least I tried.

Dear Johan,

One of the Lenten practices I miss is the veiling of the statues during Lent. Why don't we do that anymore? It was so meaningful.

Gentle Reader—

Covered statues and crucifixes that were made to look like big black or purple blobs were meaningful? More meaningful than the statues themselves? Well, to each one's own, I suppose.

In a statement dated April 1995, the then Bishop's Committee on the Liturgy responded to inquiries regarding the veiling of statues and crosses during Lent. The article concluded, "the National Conference of Catholic Bishops never voted to continue the practice of covering crosses and images and so the practice, in accord with the rubric of the Sacramentary, has not been permissible for the past twenty-five years. Individual parishes are not free to reinstate the practice on their own."

The current version of the Roman Missal, however, rectifies that situation, as a rubric for the Fifth Sunday of Lent indicates that from that Sunday on the practice of covering statues and crucifixes may be observed in the dioceses of the United States. If done, crucifixes are to remain covered until after the Celebration of the Lord's Passion on Good Friday, while statues remain covered until the beginning of the Easter Vigil.

The covering of images is rooted in the medieval tradition of visual fasting. In Germany, for example, a so-called *hungertuch* or hunger cloth was hung in front of the sanctuary, hiding the magnificent high altar from sight throughout Lent. The name "hunger cloth" does not refer to fasting from food but rather to visual fasting. This visual fasting, which was intended to cause spiritual hunger, was not from all images but rather from those images that were colorful and magnificent. Hunger cloths themselves were covered with images of Jesus and the saints, though muted and more simplistic. These were intended to inspire the faithful who gazed on them during Lent.

Another example of this kind of visual fast is the medieval custom of closing triptychs (paintings consisting of three panels) or polyptychs (paintings consisting of multiple panels). The inside of these paintings was very colorful and richly decorated. The back of the side panels had images of saints or saintly scenes that were painted in grisaille or gray tones. During penitential seasons, the side panels were shut, thus hiding the colorful inside yet revealing the images of saints, painted in grays on the outside. This allowed the faithful to meditate on the lives of the saints, while fasting from the magnificent inside. When they were reopened on Sundays and holy days, the visual hunger of people was satisfied as they gazed upon a magnificent foreshadowing of heaven.

In either case, though visually deprived from the more splendid high altar or paintings, the faithful were left with the images of the passion of Christ or of the saints so they might meditate on them and be inspired by them during their Lenten journey.

Since it is our goal—especially during Lent—to become more and more like Christ, we may be well served by meditating on the cross as well as on the lives of the saints that surround us in our church. Hiding them from sight does not necessarily support this spiritual goal.

Dear Johan,

Our seasonal décor, especially the banners, are beautiful and I know people spend lots of time and energy imagining and executing them. Yet, I am afraid I don't always understand their meaning. Is that a problem?

Gentle Reader—

Sometimes one looks for a meaning where none is intended. Just the other day I was asked about the meaning of the three gigantic purple banners that hang from the dome of our church during Lent. Surely there must be a meaning to the number three? Of course there is a meaning to the number three—for one, it is a reference to the Trinity, but to be honest, we hung three banners because it looked right. One would have been silly. Two was not quite enough and three was just right.

Sometimes colors, shapes, textures, and movement are just that—colors, shapes, textures, and movement. Still, colors add festivity or sobriety; textures add depth or transparency; shapes add interest and captivity; and movement adds life and energy . . . all characteristics of seasonal liturgy.

In addition, the colors may relate to a specific feast, season, or sacrament, for example, purple for Lent and gold for Easter, red for Passion Sunday, blue for baptism. Specific shapes may carry a specific meaning, such as a lily referring to the Blessed Virgin or to St. Joseph. Movement and textures, too, may be very liturgically specific. Thus the combination of color, shape, texture, and movement may result in the most intricate and theologically complex installation possible. Sometimes this deep meaning is known only to the creators and sometimes the meaning is grasped or new meanings are discovered by the beholder.

I remember working on a Pentecost installation in our church. We used over one thousand one-foot-square pieces of cloth in different tones of red and orange and yellow to make one giant mobile that hung in the center of the church above the assembly. The color was selected for the feast. Our hope was that the mobile would maybe look like a giant flame. In addition, we asked our families to write their names on the pieces of cloth, making the connection between our local church and the church initiated at Pentecost. Because of the air movement, the mobile continually moved like flames dancing over the assembly.

Though at first experienced by many as just another beautiful mobile, gradually it started to reveal its many layers of meaning to the community as each piece of material came to represent a member or members of our community and all pieces together represented the church.

Thus, sometimes three purple banners are just three Lenten banners that take on their own meaning, while a theologically complex mobile may at first be seen as just that before revealing itself as an image of the church, the Body of Christ, the temple of the Holy Spirit, the creative and saving hands of God in the world.

So, when you are mesmerized by banners and meditate on their meaning, just let them speak to you. Rejoice in what they have to say but if they remain silent, don't worry about it because silence was maybe what you needed.

Dear Johan,

I noticed that a new image of Our Lady of Guadalupe was installed in our church. Since our church is dedicated to Mary, we already have several depictions of her, including Our Lady of Lourdes, Our Lady of Fatima, and Our Lady of Czestochowa. Do we really need more?

Gentle Reader—

The fact that you have representations of Our Lady of Lourdes, Fatima, and Czestochowa makes me think that your church was founded by European immigrants in the late nineteenth or early twentieth century. In addition, your town must have been large enough to welcome immigrants from different European countries (France, Portugal, and Poland) yet too small to accommodate three independent national churches. By including a depiction of Mary as she appeared or is venerated in each country, immigrants from different nations were able to feel at home in one and the same church.

It is quite extraordinary that most countries and even many cities venerate a local image of Mary. Sometimes this is a statue or a painting with a long and miraculous presence in a specific locale. Sometimes it is a representation of an indigenous Marian apparition. And to be sure, these kinds of apparitions are numerous and varied. As a matter of fact, Mary has appeared in the likeness of nearly every race and culture known to Christianity.

As such Mary is not only the Queen of the Apostles but also the Queen of the Missionaries. Before the concept of inculturation was even invented, Mary wisely started to inculturate Christianity. Had it not been for Mary in her apparition as Our Lady of Guadalupe, for example, Christianity would have had a much harder time taking root in the Americas. No wonder Our Lady of Guadalupe has since been declared the patron saint of the Americas and thus shrines dedicated to her have appeared in many churches.

The face of your community, not unlike most other Catholic communities in this country, has undoubtedly changed since those founding days to include a much more diverse representation of the world church. By adding the new shrine your pastor responded to the needs of your community today in the same way as the pastor of the community did some one hundred years ago. By accommodating representations of Our Lady of Lourdes, Fatima, and Czestochowa the founding pastor made sure that everyone who worshiped in his church would feel at home and could be spiritually nourished. By adding the shrine dedicated to Our Lady of Guadalupe your current pastor is making sure that today's community feels at home and is spiritually nourished.

As to your question about the number of Marian shrines you should have and might there be too many, some would say yes. I, however, would like to offer a more nuanced answer. This is really not a numbers question. Rather, you should let yourself be guided by the needs of the community. Do all members have a sense of coming home when they enter your church? If not, no matter how many shrines it takes, by all means, build them.

Dear Johan,

I just visited a city that has two main churches. Both are quite beautiful. One is known as the basilica while the other is referred to as the cathedral. Can you tell me what the difference is between a basilica and a cathedral?

Gentle Reader—

Working in an area that has both a basilica and a cathedral and, more poignantly, working in a church that is both a basilica and a cathedral, I have answered this question numerous times.

Simply put, a cathedral is the bishop's church while a basilica is the pope's church.

When you visited the cathedral, you undoubtedly saw an over-sized chair in a prominent place in the sanctuary. It may have been elevated and perhaps it was augmented with a canopy. This chair is sometimes referred to as the episcopal throne. Borrowed from Roman imperial custom, the chair is the ancient symbol of the teaching office and the authority of the bishop. No one but the bishop is to use this chair. The Latin word for this chair is *cathedra*. It is from this Latin word that the name cathedral is derived. A cathedral thus is a church with a *cathedra* and is the church of the bishop.

The word basilica is a Latin adaptation of the Greek, meaning "hall of the king." In origin this characteristic building was a large but simple rectangular structure with a half-circle apse on one end.

The Romans readily adopted both the shape and the name from the Greeks because it worked well for their public and religious needs. When Christianity gained official status in the Roman Empire and the number of Christians quickly grew, larger buildings were needed. Bishops adopted the known and tried basilica style buildings as the architectural style for their churches. They even retained the name "basilica" because Christ is the King of all kings. A basilica thus became the hall of the King of kings.

The four major or papal basilicas in Rome (St. Peter's, St. John Lateran, St. Mary Major, St. Paul Outside-the-Walls) were constructed during Roman times. They rank among the most important churches in all of Christendom not only because of their venerable age but also because several of them house very important relics.

Today's use of the title "basilica" or, more specifically, "minor basilica" is no longer connected to an architectural style but rather is used as an honorific designation bestowed by the pope. The reason for such designation may be the fact that a church was constructed in an exquisite architectural style, is a popular place of pilgrimage, is of historic importance, has liturgical excellence, or some other reason. By bestowing the title of minor basilica on a church, the Holy Father, in a certain sense, attaches this church to his own household. A basilica therefore is the pope's church in a given area.

In addition to a coat of arms, the insignia of a basilica are the *tintinnabulum* or silver bell and the *ombrellino* or half-opened pavilion. Both are said to have been used when the pope traveled through Rome to visit a church. The bell was carried at the beginning of the procession to announce to the people that a papal procession was about to pass by. At the receiving church the youngest cleric was charged with watching for the arriving procession. He is said to have held an umbrella in half-open position so he was at the ready. As soon as he saw the pope he was to run to him while completely opening the umbrella to protect the pope from sun or rain. The *ombrellino* is now half open as a sign that a basilica is waiting for the visit of the pope.

Today there are seventy-four minor basilicas in the United States. The Basilica of Saint Mary in Minneapolis was the first church in the United States to be granted this title when on February 2, 1926, Pope Pius XI made it so.

Dear Johan,

I drove by your church the other night and I noticed a bonfire outside. I could see it from the highway. I know you do many strange things but what is that all about?

Gentle Reader—

I presume you are referring to the Easter fire. This is indeed somewhat of an unusual rite, even for us Catholics. As it is celebrated outside, it often causes passing traffic to slow down. I know of at least a couple accidents due to curious gawking. And one time the fire department arrived during the blessing of the fire. For full disclosure, I work in a downtown church and our fire pit is twelve feet wide. I am sure this would not happen were we to use the customary, yet regrettable, mini-barbeque.

The Easter fire, not unlike some other Christian rituals, is pagan in origin. In this case it is a ritual rooted in the Saxon custom of lighting fires to mark the passing of the seasons. This was done in celebration of the returning of light at the spring equinox and the fullness of light during the summer solstice. Though not as popular, it was also done occasionally in mourning for the diminishing of light at the fall equinox and to break the depth of darkness at the time of the winter solstice.

The fire lit to mark the spring equinox was the most popular. Not only did it allow for a celebration of the end of winter and the return of light but it also had very practical implications. All the unwanted vegetation was burned in the bonfires. The resulting ashes were used as a fertilizer for the fields. Thus these spring fires symbolize light, help with cleansing, and result in increased fertility.

Christians could easily "baptize" this ritual as the season of Lent and Easter clearly is about cleansing, light, and fertility. The Lenten exercises are intended as a spiritual cleansing. During the Easter Vigil we celebrate Christ as the Light of the World. And from the baptismal waters new Christians arise. All this is celebrated and anticipated with the Easter fire.

Just as an aside, given your interest in fires, there is another day during the liturgical year that we light fires. Though much less common, there is a custom to light fires on the eve of the feast of St. John the Baptist, which falls on June 24. These fires are known as St. John's fires. They too are a Christianized version of the Saxon solstice fires that preceded them.

Next time you see the Easter fire, why not stop and check it out?

Liturgical Prayer and Devotions

Dear Johan,

Our pastor announces Sunday Vespers every week. Why doesn't he tell us what they are? We might be more inclined to go if we knew. So I ask you: What are they?

Gentle Reader—

I am not sure if describing Vespers will make you want to go. It might all sound a bit boring to you. My recommendation would be that you just go and experience Vespers before you read this column. You might really enjoy it.

Vespers, also known as evening prayer, needs to be understood in the context of the desire of Christians, in keeping with Jewish custom and the Pauline exhortation to "Pray without ceasing" (1 Thess 5:17; Eph 6:18). As a result we have marked the different segments of a day with prayers, ever since apostolic times. The earliest evidence of organized daily morning and evening prayer dates back to the third century.

With the increase of monastic fervor, the frequency of daily gatherings for prayer increased. Some monastic communities' charism was to dedicate themselves entirely to praising God and sanctifying the successive moments of day and night in communal prayer. Saint Benedict, for example, asked of his monks that they recite all 150 psalms in a week. More fervent monks even recited all 150 psalms each day. This form of prayer is known as Liturgy of the Hours or the Divine Office.

Lay Christians and parish priests who were unable to tend to their prayer life twenty-four hours a day lived out the call to prayer in a different way. They marked fewer but set moments of the day with prayer, either in private or in community. Three times each day: at the rising of the sun, at midday, and at the setting of the sun the local church bells invited people to stop working and pray for just a few moments. This prayer is known as the *Angelus*. Many churches still ring their bells at those times but few people respond to them.

The prayer of clerics was and is a bit more involved. They observe three major times of prayer (the Office of Readings, Lauds, and Vespers) and two minor times of prayer (midday prayer and Compline). Lauds is Latin for praise, for indeed in the morning praise is to be given for the new day. The Office of Readings precedes Lauds. Vespers is derived from the Latin for evening star. A major element of Vespers is the blessing of the light. The middle of the day is marked by a relatively short midday prayer. The day concludes with night prayer or Compline, which is Latin for completion.

Each one of these prayer times ordinarily consists of a hymn of praise, psalm(s) and/or canticle(s), a brief reading from Scripture, and a series of intercessory prayers that are concluded with the Lord's Prayer.

Today, St. Paul's exhortation to "pray without ceasing" is mostly ignored by the majority of Christians as we busy ourselves with many other things. It may be good to reintroduce regular moments of prayer into our lives. Sunday Vespers may not be a bad start and please do listen for the bells.

Dear Johan,

I am somewhat confused by the fact that we call Mary Mother of God. Would it not be better to refer to her as the Mother of Jesus?

Gentle Reader—

Be careful, someone may accuse you of Nestorianism and St. Gregory of Nazianzus (ca. 329–90) would have replied that if you question that Mary is the Mother of God, you are at odds with God. In your defense, this is a matter that took a few centuries to settle.

The title of Mother of God, or *Theotokos* in Greek, is one of the oldest titles for Mary. The earliest written references date back to the early third century and by the fourth century the use of the title was widespread. This does not mean, however, that the theology of this title was fully developed. It also does not mean that the title was accepted by all.

Indicative of this ongoing discovery of the meaning of the title *Theotokos* is the conflict that arose in Constantinople between those who insisted on the title *Theotokos* or "God-bearer," emphasizing that in Christ God had been born as a human, and those who rejected that title because God as an eternal being could not have been born. Nestorius, who was patriarch of Constantinople between 428 and 431, tried to find a middle ground and suggested the title of *Christotokos* or Christ-bearer. Neither camp accepted this title.

In order to once and for all settle the debate Cyril of Alexandria (ca. 376–444) and Celestine of Rome (422–32) called on Emperor Theodosius II (401–50) to call an ecumenical council. During this somewhat unruly council, known as the First Council of Ephesus (431), Nestorius was condemned for suggesting that the title *Christotokos* was preferable over *Theotokos*. Since Nestorius was unwilling to recant, he was deposed and banned.

From that time onward, the church in both the East and West has embraced the title of *Theotokos*, thus emphasizing the divine nature of Jesus even when human.

So, are you OK with using the title? Or will you continue to teeter on the brink of Nestorian heresy?

Dear Johan,

My mother used to drag us to novenas when we were young. Whatever happened to them? They seem to have disappeared.

Gentle Reader—

I grew up with them too. The one I remember the best is the novena to St. Anthony, the Wonderworker. My grandmother had a great devotion to St. Anthony and was in regular need of his help with lost items. At her instigation my father took my brother and me to our local Franciscan friary for the yearly novena of St. Anthony. This meant that for nine Tuesdays leading up to the feast of St. Anthony on June 13, the day of his *dies natalis* or the day of his birth into heaven, we went to early morning Mass with the friars. I don't remember much about what we did except that we attended Mass, prayed a special prayer, and brought white lilies, which I was told were St. Anthony's favorite flowers. As a treat we had breakfast at my grandmother's home rather than at ours.

The word novena comes from the Latin word *novem*, meaning nine. Thus a novena is a series of nine days on which one prays for a specific need. Usually these are nine consecutive days. So, the novena for the gifts of the Holy Spirit, for example, is prayed on the nine days leading up to Pentecost, starting on the Friday of the sixth week of Easter and ending on the Saturday of the seventh week of Easter. In those churches that still celebrate the Ascension of the Lord on the Thursday between the sixth and seventh Sundays of Easter, the novena for the gifts of the Holy

Spirit is prayed on the nine days between Ascension Thursday and Pentecost Sunday.

A novena can also be prayed on the same day of the week for nine consecutive weeks. This is the case with the novena of St. Anthony.

Like many other traditional devotions, novenas have largely fallen to the wayside in the Western world. Thankfully, in other parts of the world these and other devotions are practiced with great fervor. New immigrants often bring these with them and thus they are gradually being reintroduced in parts of the church where they are dormant.

So, if you miss praying novenas, why don't you go in search for one or, better yet, maybe your pastor might be willing to start one. I would start slowly by suggesting a novena for the gifts of the Holy Spirit. How could he say no?

Dear Johan,

I just returned from Europe. The number of relics I saw was astounding. And some were rather gruesome. It made me uncomfortable. Why do we (they) have them?

Gentle Reader—

I agree, visiting the shrines of the saints throughout Europe is not for the faint of heart. By contrast to the United States, where the relics are mostly small and discreetly enshrined in reliquaries, Europeans proudly display entire bodies or recognizable body parts of saints for veneration. I vividly remember visiting the shrine of St. Roseline de Villeneuve near Draguignan in France. The body of the saint is displayed in the center of the shrine. Because she was a celebrated visionary, her eyes were removed upon her death and set in a separate reliquary. Other memorable relics are the tongue and vocal cords of St. Anthony on display in the basilica dedicated to the saint in Padua, and the finger of St. Catherine on display in Siena, to name but a few.

The veneration of relics is rooted in the cult of the saints, which is so dear to Catholics. The martyrs were the first to be recognized as saints. Their willingness to die for Christ was seen as the greatest possible sacrifice. Thus their memory was honored and their bodies were treated with the greatest respect. Their tombs were marked and, over time, were decorated. Christians desired to be buried as close as possible to the martyrs. The thinking was that at the end of time, when Christ returned to judge both the living and the dead, those who were closest to the martyrs would somehow share in their glory and be swooped into heaven in their wake.

As Christianity spread Christians still desired to be close to their beloved saints. So, they took pieces of cloth that touched the saint's body or even pieces of the body itself with them. They buried these relics in their altars, placed them in their homes, and wore them around their necks. Gradually, protective powers were accorded to the relics of martyrs and saints. Many miracle stories testify to this. The most powerful relics were even fought over.

Today, relics are revered as tangible reminders of the saints whose memory we honor. As is the case with images of the saints, we do not worship the relics themselves but rather the persons they represent. Their stories reflect the different ways in which we can live out our calling as Christians to become more like Christ in our world.

I truly hope that your encounter with the relics of the saints did not prevent you from learning about them. If it did, I invite you to return to those places and, after having gotten over your initial shock, to allow the saints to speak to you about the ways in which they answered their individual callings. Who knows, you may learn a thing or two about your own. And that is what this is all about.

Dear Johan,

When I was in Amiens, France, I saw the head of John the Baptist. I have since discovered that several other locations claim to possess his severed head. What's going on?

Gentle Reader—

Named one of the top ten religious relics in the world by *Time* magazine in 2010, the true whereabouts of the head of John the Baptist is uncertain. Many places claim to have the remains of John the Baptist in their care. According to the Orthodox Church John's relics are preserved among other places on Mount Athos and on St. Ivan Island in Bulgaria. The Roman Catholic Church reveres a skull said to be of John the Baptist in *San Silvestro in Capite* in Rome and in the Cathedral of Amiens, to name but two. Even the Muslim world lays claim to the remains of this saint they honor as a prophet. Thus there is a shrine to him in the Umayyad Mosque in Damascus, Syria, and in the Topkapı Palace in Istanbul, Turkey.

Ordinarily there is no issue with the relics of a saint being found in different locations, as different parts of different saints are available for veneration in different churches. The issue with St. John is that all the remains together do not add up to just one body.

Forensic research, which has been allowed on some relics, has shown that some of them might indeed be of St. John since they are of a man roughly from the same place and time when John the Baptist lived. However, put together there are too many parts and the different parts do not all match. For example, the lower jaw that is said to be of St. John and is kept in Verdun does not prove to be a match to the skull kept in Amiens that is missing the lower jaw.

So, from a historical and scientific point of view it is clear that not all of these relics are indeed St. John's. It is not even entirely clear if any of these are the true relics since all of them have somewhat of an abstruse history. The Orthodox Church even has a feast dedicated to the first and second findings of the head of John the Baptist on February 24 and another feast dedicated to the third finding of the head of St. John on May 25.

Like with all relics, we need to approach the relics of St. John from a place of faith. In the end, we do not worship the relics themselves; rather we honor the memory of the saint they represent. The tangible remains allow us to remember the lives of the saints. They invite us to be inspired by their deep faith. They encourage us to ask God for the strength to be more like them, our heroes in the faith.

So, go ahead and kiss the skull of St. John the Baptist when it is presented for veneration on the feast of the decapitation on August 29 in the Cathedral of Amiens. But when you kiss the skull, remember that it is the saint you honor and not just the skull you kiss, which may or may not be his.

Dear Johan,

A friend made fun of me for having a medal of St. Christopher in my car. He said that Christopher did not even exist. Is that true? Should I get rid of the medal?

Gentle Reader—

When I was growing up we had images of St. Christopher everywhere. My father insisted on having a magnetic image of Christopher stuck to the dashboard of his car. My mom always made sure a medal of St. Christopher was pinned to the inside of my suitcase whenever I left for an overnight. And my grandmother reserved a place of honor for St. Christopher in her home, right next to

St. Anthony. When she knew I was traveling she put St. Christopher in front of St. Anthony, almost in line with the Blessed Virgin herself, and lit an extra candle.

This all happened in the late sixties and early seventies. At that time we were blissfully unaware that Christopher had been quietly removed from the Roman calendar of saints but was retained in the Roman Martyrology, which contains the list of all the known martyrs and saints. I suspect many of us are unaware of this even today. No matter, since we can still honor him as a saint in our local churches and in our daily devotions.

Very little is known about Christopher. The Roman Martyrology simply mentions that he was martyred for the faith in Lycia during the reign of Roman emperor Decius (249–51). The *Golden Legend*, a thirteenth-century compilation of the lives of saints and their miracles, gives a little more information about St. Christopher. The popular depiction of the saint crossing a river while carrying the Christ Child is based on the *Golden Legend*. Christopher was asked by a monk to serve Christ by helping pilgrims cross a strong river. One day he crossed the river carrying a small child on his shoulders. As he made his way the water became very turbulent and the child very heavy. After a great struggle he made it to the other side. Christopher told the child that he felt like he had carried the entire weight of the world on his shoulders. The child replied that he carried much more than that: the very Creator of that world. Then the child disappeared. Christopher went on to preach the Gospel and ultimately gave his life for the faith.

Regarding St. Christopher's medal in your car, I would suggest you keep it. On the one hand, it is a visual reminder of our calling as Christians to bring Christ to the world. The name Christopher or *Christophoros* in Greek literally means Christ-bearer. As Christians we are all called to be *Christophoroi* or Christ-bearers; in other words, we are to bring Christ to the world. On the other hand, whenever we ask for a saint's assistance, we ultimately ask for God's assistance. And who can fault us for that?

Dear Johan,

I am a new Catholic. When I went to Mass today, the priest placed candles around people's throats while he was whispering something I could not understand. I found it strange and decided not to participate. I am still getting used to all this stuff.

Gentle Reader—

As your Catholic journey continues, you will undoubtedly happen upon more of these ritual surprises. They make Catholicism interesting.

You must have gone to church on February 3, the feast of St. Blaise, a fourth-century bishop and martyr. On that day we have the traditional blessing of the throats. This is what the priest said while he placed the candles around people's throats: "Through the intercession of Saint Blaise, bishop and martyr, may God deliver you from every disease of the throat and any other illness. In the name of the Father and of the Son and of the Holy Spirit" (Order for the Blessing of Throats on the Feast of Saint Blaise, chap. 51 in *Book of Blessings*).

The little we know about St. Blaise comes from descriptions of the lives of saints that were written several centuries after his death. From these writings we learn that Blaise was a celebrated medical doctor when he was elected as bishop of Sebastea, Armenia, today's Sivas, Turkey. He was brutally martyred around 316 during a wave of Christian persecution.

From the sixth century on in the East and the eighth century in the West the intercession of St. Blaise was invoked by people who were ill. By the twelfth century St. Blaise had become one of the most popular saints in Western Europe.

Two stories told about St. Blaise relate to the custom of blessing throats. According to the first story a distraught mother rushed her child to St. Blaise. The child was choking on a fishbone. After St. Blaise said a prayer the fishbone dislodged and the child was saved. Based on this miracle, the intercession of St. Blaise is invoked when suffering from ailments of the throat as well as to prevent such ailments.

According to the second story a poor widow's pig had been saved from a wolf by St. Blaise. Out of gratitude, the widow brought two candles to prison so St. Blaise could have some light in his dark cell. Blaise is often depicted with two candles held together by a red ribbon. The red ribbon refers to the martyrdom suffered by St. Blaise. Two candles tied together with a red ribbon are used during the blessing of the throats.

Even in our postmodern society, which is suspicious of any hint of superstition, this blessing, like many other similar rites, remains popular among Catholics. They are the visible signs of a deep yet invisible reality. The blessing of the throats is a tangible reminder of God's healing and saving presence among us. It is also an acknowledgment that we entrust ourselves to God's providential care.

So, here you have it. Are you ready to try it next year?

Dear Johan,

We love celebrating the Stations of the Cross, especially during Lent. However, some of our friends seem to think that this is an old-fashioned custom and should be abolished. What do you think?

Gentle Reader—

Stations of the Cross, one of the most popular devotional practices of the Catholic Church, is indeed, like many other aspects of our faith, loved by some and belittled by others.

Regardless of one's affection for the practice, its fundamental concept of a spiritual journey through the last days of Jesus' life is rooted in a deep human need to see, touch, and experience places of personal, historic, or religious importance. Sometimes people will travel thousands of miles to visit such places. Catholic football fans, for instance, will think nothing of crossing the country merely to visit the football stadium at Notre Dame and to touch the statue of Knute Rockne. Most Catholics have a pilgrimage to Rome, Lourdes, or the Holy Land on their bucket list. Muslims, Jews, and Christians alike visit Jerusalem, an important location on the spiritual map of these three major monotheistic religions.

This desire to visit Jerusalem is nothing new. During the Middle Ages, western European Christians not only desired to visit the places where Jesus had lived but also to defend them from non-Christians. Thus, some medieval Christians went to Jerusalem as pilgrims, others as crusaders. Regardless of their intent, those who returned to their homelands brought back stories and descriptions of the holy sites.

The growing emphasis on the Lord's passion during a time plagued with pestilence, famine, and war, combined with the pilgrim stories, gave rise to the creation of shrines dedicated to the passion of our Lord. Preached by the Franciscan Friars, a devotion that followed Jesus on his last journey from his trial to his tomb developed.

Today's Stations of the Cross are characterized as a meditation on Jesus' obedience unto death, God's unending love, and our human frailty. Lent, with its baptismal and penitential emphasis, is well suited for the celebration of this devotion.

Though we may think that we have always celebrated the Stations of the Cross in the same ways, they have actually varied greatly over time and they continue to do so. The most recent version of the Stations of the Cross was introduced by Pope John Paul II on Good Friday 1991. This version differs both in content and in number from the traditional fourteen stations. In terms of content, Pope John Paul's individual stations are all based on the Scriptures. Such stations as "Jesus meets Veronica," which has no biblical reference, have been replaced. In terms of number, John Paul II added one more station: the resurrection.

In the end, more important than the number or the theme of the stations is the intent of the people who enter into this devotion and how this devotion changes their lives into becoming more like Christ, the giver of life.

And please tell your friend that *no*, I don't think it should be abolished. Even if I did, I know it will not.

Dear Johan,

Blessing of the animals? I had never heard of such a thing and all of a sudden everyone seems to do it. Can you say something about this? I fear this might be sacrilegious.

Gentle Reader—

If only you could have experienced my first blessing of animals. You would surely not write the way you just did.

I was in Assisi at the Franciscan monastery of San Damiano on the feast of St. Francis. Some of the neighboring farmers joined us for the celebration of the Eucharist. To my surprise, they brought all sorts of animals. The early October weather was glorious and the Eucharist we celebrated in the courtyard of the monastery was unforgettable. Being a romantic, I saw myself in Zeffirelli's movie *Brother Sun, Sister Moon*. I will never forget the experience.

Since that time I have learned that Catholics bless all sorts of things. We even have a rather substantial book that gives direction to these blessings: the Catholic *Book of Blessings*. If you were surprised by the blessing of animals, you might even be more startled by other blessings in the book: athletic fields, all sorts of machinery, fishing gear, motorbikes, shopping malls, and communications centers, to name just a few. Catholics like to bless things.

The English verb "to bless" is derived from the Middle English word *blessen*, which in turn comes from the Old English *bletsian*, which has *blod*, meaning blood, as its root, referring to the use of blood in an act of consecration. Although no longer through the usage of blood, creation is lifted up before God and hallowed during the blessing. In Latin the verb is *benedicere*, from *bene* and *dicere*: to speak well or to speak words of good omen.

In sum, when we bless someone or something, we engage in a twofold action: first, we bless and thank God for the many gifts bestowed on us; second, we ask God to hallow that which is being blessed. Therefore, when we bless animals—recognizing their sacred place in creation—we thank God for the gift of animals and we ask God to protect them. This is a most sacred, and assuredly not a sacrilegious, act.

May I suggest you put the *Book of Blessings* on your wish list?

Dear Johan,

What is your thinking on religious processions such as rosary processions and Corpus Christi processions? I used to enjoy them but now they make me somewhat uncomfortable.

Gentle Reader—

Having grown up in a Catholic country, I cannot imagine the Catholic landscape without religious parades and processions. I simply love religious pageantry and outdoor expressions of our faith, which over the centuries have been adopted by many different cultures in many varied ways. As a result we have a myriad of processions. In addition to the ones you mention, we have the passion processions during Holy Week, processions with relics on the feasts of the saints, processions to the cemetery, outdoor Stations of the Cross, and so forth. Processions are a great example of popular Catholicism.

One very notable procession is the silent procession (stille omgang) in Amsterdam, The Netherlands. The origin is a eucharistic miracle that took place during the Middle Ages. As a result, Amsterdam became a place of pilgrimage and a solemn procession was held every year to mark the miracle. When Amsterdam officially became Protestant in 1578, Catholicism was banished and Catholics either converted or went underground worshiping in hidden churches. After Catholicism became legal again in the nineteenth century, the procession to celebrate the eucharistic miracle was reinstituted. Since then, the procession has been held as a silent march not only celebrating the miracle but also testifying to the persecution of the Catholic Church, which was overcome.

Having lived in the northern parts of the United States for many years, my thinking about processions has been challenged and as a result is no longer as clear-cut as it used to be. I still value processions, but have some concerns about them as well.

On the one hand, it is important to tend to these ancient customs and exhibit our faith to the world. Processions in a sense are a visual testimony to our faith. They provide us with evangelizing tools that sometimes speak more effectively than any sermon or theological discourse could do.

On the other hand, we have to face the reality that this behavior might encourage religious anger and even violence. In our very diverse religious landscape, procession might be seen as flaunting our own religion. Of course, one would expect tolerance for legitimate spiritual activities of all religions, but does that hold when put on display on city streets? I expect that religious processions of all kinds are great, as long as they are done in a spirit of prayer and devotion, and not in order to make a politico-religious statement.

I am not sure this will have alleviated your discomfort, but maybe that is not a bad thing.

Dear Johan,

I think every parish should have perpetual adoration, but our pastor refuses. His excuse is that we are not set up for it. Moreover, he argues, since the Blessed Sacrament is reserved in the tabernacle in the church, there is nothing to stop people from praying there. I think that's a cop-out. Do you think I should go to the bishop?

Gentle Reader—

What has become of us? Does everything have to be a power struggle? Please do not go to the bishop, but rather in all humility continue your conversation with your pastor.

This kind of situation often happens when we cannot see the liturgical forest for the trees or even the one tree. Your quest for perpetual adoration cannot be undertaken in a vacuum fanned by the temptation of a divisive and regrettable one-issue mentality. Rather I would advocate for a much broader approach in which perpetual adoration may or may not have a place depending on the specific circumstances of your parish.

Let me start by assuring you that devotion to the Real Presence of Christ in the Blessed Sacrament is an essential part of our Catholic faith. It is necessarily rooted in and directed toward an ever deeper relationship with Christ. Unless this relationship exists, all the rest is nothing but intellectual gymnastics and ritualistic posturing.

The celebration of the Eucharist is undeniably the primary locus of our encounter with Christ and, therefore, of the greatest importance for the development of our relationship with Christ. In the Eucharist we encounter Christ in the assembly gathered for prayer, in the celebrating priest, in the word of God that is proclaimed, and in the Body and Blood of Christ broken and poured out for us. The culmination of the Eucharist and the apex of the encounter with the Body of Christ happen at the time of Communion. That is why ample time for silent prayer following

Communion is strongly encouraged. Flowing from this encounter with Christ in the Eucharist is a desire to be ever closer to Christ. It is this desire that calls us back to church Sunday after Sunday and sometimes day after day. It is this desire that also calls us to pray the Liturgy of the Hours and to engage in eucharistic and other devotions. Because of their closeness to the celebration of the Eucharist, eucharistic devotions such as adoration and benediction are the highest among all devotions and should be engaged in regularly.

At the same time as our liturgical encounters with Christ nourish our relationship with him, study of the Scriptures and tradition ought to deepen our knowledge of him, which in turn makes our liturgical encounters more fruitful.

Nourished by the Eucharist and inspired by our studies, we are sent out to encounter the Body of Christ in our poor, broken, and often hurting world.

The task of your pastor is to balance all this and to make sure that the Body of Christ is encountered in the Eucharist and related prayer, is contemplated through the study of Scripture and tradition, and is honored through service of the Body of Christ in the world. Perpetual adoration may or may not fit in this overall plan for your particular church. If it does, that is great. If it doesn't, the lack of perpetual adoration in and of itself does not make your parish less Catholic. After all, even Jesus did not call for it. He did, however, command us to celebrate the Eucharist and to wash one another's feet.

Dear Johan,

February 2 fell on a Sunday this year and I experienced the feast of the Presentation in the Temple for the first time. The blessing of the light was beautiful. What does it all mean?

Gentle Reader—

I agree, this is a lovely celebration. I wish it fell on a Sunday every year.

When I was growing up we always attended early morning Eucharist on that day. Upon entering the church, we received a candle, one per family. After the priest said a prayer and sprinkled holy water, we walked around the church in procession. As the oldest child I was tasked with carrying our family's candle. My current fondness of processions probably dates back to those times when I carried the candle under the watchful eye of my parents and the envious glances of my siblings. After the Eucharist we were encouraged to take our candle home and to care for it with reverence. The priest told us to light the candle in times of need. I distinctly remember lighting our candle while we prayed for my great-grandfather who was mortally ill. We also found some solace in this candle once he died. We even would light the candle and huddle around it during bad storms. It made us less afraid.

Many years later, when living in a Benedictine abbey, we celebrated the day with even greater ceremony as the candles were bigger, the procession was longer, and the sung psalms were more numerous. I can still hear the sounds, see the sights, and smell the burning wax that even overpowered the copious amounts of incense used for the procession.

Memories are great yet they need to be interpreted carefully. My childhood experience of the feast reveals profound truths but maybe there was a hint of superstition that tainted the use of the candles at home. Or was it the result of a more generous and less

complicated faith? My monastic memories, again revelatory of
deep faith, undoubtedly suffer from some liturgical romanticism.

The essence of the feast is this: Christ is the Light of the world
and we are to witness to the Light in word and deed. The candles
are a tangible symbol of the light of Christ. And the procession is
not just a pretty parade; rather it symbolizes and rehearses us in
our calling to bring Christ's light to the world.

As a child I always wished we could keep the candle burning
throughout the liturgy and even on our way home. I did not quite
know why but I thought it made sense. I still imagine this grand
procession of all Christians leaving their respective churches on
the feast of the Presentation of the Lord, or any feast for that matter, with lit candle in hand, proclaiming to the world that Christ is
the Light and we bear witness to him in word and deed.

Liturgical Diversity
and Inclusivity

Dear Johan,

Although I am not an extreme feminist, I am often struck by the woman-unfriendly language used in the liturgy. What can be done?

Gentle Reader—

I am reminded of the procession of Echternach, Luxembourg, when thinking of liturgical language. That procession is known for the fact that everyone participating makes three steps forward followed by two steps backward followed by three steps forward, and so on. I have the impression that the same is happening in our church when it comes to inclusive language. We take three steps forward followed by two steps backward, or is it two steps forward followed by three steps backward? And, of course, the slow progress we experience in the church is exasperated by the fact that day-to-day language has long since resolved the issue.

Our God, who invites all, is not served by a language that alienates many. It is therefore vital that the liturgy, in its language, its music, and its rituals, be inclusive of all people it desires to reach.

When looking at the liturgical texts, both spoken and sung, one must distinguish between horizontal language and vertical language. The latter either addresses God or speaks about God, while the former deals with humans. Horizontal language is a rather easy problem to fix and there really is no excuse why it should not happen. The God language is much more delicate, complicated, and politically sensitive.

The power of language to heal and destroy is all too often underestimated. Language is not simply an intellectual exercise; it is wrought with feelings and emotions that should not be neglected or trampled upon.

I could venture to guess why the church continues to insist on using so-called exclusive language even when referring to humans; however, that would be neither prudent nor wise. So, my suggestion to you is to wait patiently and to ask your question again and again and again.

Dear Johan,

I get so tired of people wanting to change the word of God. I find it even bordering on the sacrilegious. This is the word of God we are talking about. Can't they just leave it alone?

Gentle Reader—

Honestly, I am convinced some people think the word of God came to us in English.

The answer to your question is simple: no, we can't! Unless all of us are willing to learn the languages through which the word of God was first revealed, we will have to continue to battle with the complexities of translation. And anyone who has ever translated a text realizes that this is not a simple matter. Moreover, if translating a contemporary text from one living language into another is not an easy task, then consider the translation of a text that was written some two thousand years ago in a language that is no longer commonly used.

We also need to consider that English is blessed with a specific curse. It is a rather easy language because its operative vocabulary is not that vast. Yet it is complex because one word can mean several things depending on its context. A simple example: when the word *men* is written on the door of a certain room, it means males only. However, when we read that Jesus died for the salvation of men, it means both male and female. Now, how confusing is that?

Other languages do not have this problem or, dare I say, have evolved into no longer having this problem. In Dutch, for example, the word *man* (singular) or *mannen* (plural), meaning man, exclusively refers to males. When referring to both men and women, the word *mens* (singular) or *mensen* (plural) is used. Although the etymology of the word *mens* (human) is the same as the word *man* (man), they both have come to mean something very different and one would not interchange their usage, mistakenly claiming that the one covers the other.

Trying to understand and effectively translate the word of God is a very complicated matter. Sadly enough, those who take this very seriously are often accused of disrespect for the word of God. In addition, language, especially inclusive language, has become a source of division between different factions in the church and is seen as a barometer of orthodoxy and allegiance to the church.

Let us never forget that the word of God is living and active within the church and throughout the world. The word of God is not defined by and contained within any language, be it venerable and dead or raucous and alive. When we find ourselves before the throne of God, at the end of time, may we not find ourselves accused of stifling the living word of God.

Dear Johan,

I wish we would use more Latin in the liturgy. Not only is it the language the church has used from the beginning, it is such a worthy and venerable language. To be honest, I find English quite pedantic and not worthy of the liturgy.

Gentle Reader—

Your premise is both correct and false. You are correct to suggest that Latin is an old language. However, it is not the language the church has used from the beginning and linguists would more than likely take issue with such nomenclatures as worthy and venerable. Since English is not my mother tongue, I will not even touch on the last part of your question, or was it rather a statement?

Although Latin is still considered the premier liturgical language in the Roman Catholic Church, it has not always been that way. As a matter of fact, Latin, which was known as the *lingua vulgaris* or the language of the common people, was adopted by the church because the majority of the people were unable to understand the earlier language of the church, which was Greek.

As Christianity spread throughout the Western empire, the new language of the church and of the state, that is, Latin, went with it. After the collapse of the empire, the church held on to the rites and rubrics it had developed during Roman times. Many of those rites and rubrics as well as the liturgical language (Latin) survive until this very day.

When the church fathers of the Second Vatican Council decided to allow people to use vernacular languages to celebrate the liturgy, they actually did what our Christian ancestors had done when switching from Greek (the language of the elite) to Latin (the language of the people). The main motivator, both then and now, was that people should be able to understand what is said and done during the liturgy.

Is Latin a worthier and more venerable language? It surely is venerable due to the longevity of its use. I am not sure that makes it worthier, though. Regardless, unless people know Latin, I see absolutely no reason why a presumed esthetic quality should override intelligibility.

Dear Johan,

Why do you think our pastor allows for Latin Vespers to be sung? I thought we had gotten rid of all that in light of Vatican II. Is this yet another setback?

Gentle Reader—

Let's not come to grandiose conclusions based on the initiative of one pastor. And just for the record, although in light of the Second Vatican Council the celebration of the liturgy happens ordinarily in the vernacular language, Gregorian chant is still considered the premier form of Catholic liturgical music.

Also it seems like Gregorian chant is more popular than ever. CDs of chanting monks and nuns have popped up everywhere. Concerts featuring Gregorian chant are rather fashionable. I have even noticed my church-hesitant friends succumbing to an occasional dabble in Gregorian chant, though they may not quite know what it is.

So, if indeed people respond positively to Gregorian chant, why would we not use it in the liturgy? Of course, this needs to be done with the greatest care and sensitivity to the liturgical competence and needs of individual parishes.

This is by no means a plea for a reform-of-the-reform or a return to pre–Vatican II situations. And it is surely not an argument in favor of the expansion of the use of the so-called Tridentine Mass. It simply is an affirmation of Gregorian chant as a valid and proven form of liturgical music that may spiritually move certain people in certain situations.

As the stewards of liturgical music, we ought to be open to all the voices of our rich tradition while we actively invite new expressions that speak of and to our own times. And herein lies the key—we ought to be open to both. Too often it is one or the other. Gregorian chant should not push out all other valid liturgical expressions and neither should Gregorian chant be pushed out. We are the richer for the presence of all.

So, in the spirit of ongoing *aggiornamento* I encourage you to be open-minded and participate in Gregorian Vespers someday. It may not be your thing, as it is not most people's thing. However, it might give you a better understanding of its place within the colorful musical tapestry of our church.

Dear Johan,

We have been using the new translation of the Mass for a while now. I have to tell you, I still don't like it. Do you think we may ever go back to the old one? Maybe just in our own parish?

Gentle Reader—

I hear your frustration loud and clear and, dare I say, you are not the only one who feels this way.

To put my answer into context, let's do a brief historical recap. In 1970, Pope Paul VI promulgated the first post–Vatican II edition of the *Missale Romanum, editio typica*. This official Latin version of the revised liturgy was then translated into the different vernacular languages. By 1973 the English translation of the complete Missal was ready for use in English-speaking countries. The Latin edition was already amended in 1975 by Paul VI. A translation of the 1975 edition of the Missal was immediately begun.

Before the new translation of the 1975 Missal of Paul VI was recognized for use, Pope John Paul II announced his intention to promulgate his own version of the Missal, thus rendering the translation of the 1975 Missal useless. In the year 2000 John Paul II promulgated his own Missal. He commissioned a translation according to a new set of translation guidelines and following a new process. Of note is that the new guidelines required a translation that is closer to the Latin text in a "high" language that is said to be more suitable for liturgical use than the one used for the previous translation.

On the First Sunday of Advent 2011 we finally started to use the Missal of John Paul II, which even before the translation was completed had been amended by John Paul II himself as well as by Benedict XVI.

Admittedly, the change from texts that had become "second nature" to texts that are unfamiliar and seem somewhat strange has not been easy. All change is difficult; change in the liturgy is even more difficult because we love our liturgy and take our liturgy very seriously. The process of switching from one translation to another is almost like mourning the death of a loved family member. In order to process the loss we have to work through several stages of feelings ranging from grief to anger to acceptance.

Though the prayers still seem strange and forced, though people and priests alike stumble over the words, though some of us, myself included, inadvertently forget about the changes and revert to the old text out of habit, I suspect that one day the current text will be as familiar as the old. And when the time comes for us to learn yet another new translation of the Roman Missal, we may be equally upset, or not.

In the meantime, individual parishes do not have the option to return to the old translation. These have been happily or, as the case may be, unhappily retired.

With regard to the broader question about the church as a whole returning to the old translation I must respond in the negative as well. But, don't despair. Because despite what people may think, in our church change is the norm. It may be slow, but our church is marked by change nonetheless. So before we know it, we will be presented with a new translation. My suggestion to you is rather than looking backward, let's look forward.

Dear Johan,

My pastor keeps telling us that we are a diverse community, so then why is it that all the people in our windows look Caucasian, including Mary and Jesus? I find it offensive.

Gentle Reader—

Thank you for your very pertinent query. A simple answer is that descendants of Caucasian immigrants must have built your church and gave it its very European appearance. Now that we are becoming a wonderful reflection of the rich diversity of our world church, this appearance, rightfully, is being questioned.

Growing up in Belgium I imagined Mary and Jesus having blond hair and blue eyes. Not surprisingly, I was surrounded by their blond-haired and blue-eyed depictions, which looked very much like members of my own family. It was not until I became a teenager that I realized that in real life, Mary and Jesus more than likely had neither.

People of all ages and of all times have tended to visualize their God (or gods) with the imagery that is typical for their own culture. This is known as the visual inculturation of religion. In other words, the religious narrative that is cross-cultural is told in the visual images of the local culture. If you look, for instance, at the medieval depiction of Mary in the Low Countries, you will see that she is sitting in a period décor and is wearing period clothes. The same Mary painted in the Baroque period in Spain appears as a Spanish baroque Queen. Our Lady of Guadalupe is an Aztec princess, while Our Lady of La Vang appeared as a Hue woman in Vietnam. It is not until very recently that Mary and Jesus are seen in depictions that reflect their Jewish ancestry.

There is nothing wrong with this process of visual inculturation, which nurtures a sense of self-identification with the Christian narrative. The problem arises, however, when one dominant culture imposes its own "inculturated" image on another culture.

European missionaries or immigrants, for instance, often took European Christian images with them on their voyages so that it was not uncommon to find a seventeenth-century French-looking image of a Jewish Mother and Child located in a church in Vietnam.

Thankfully, as the religious imagination has changed from provincial to global, the religious representations of Christianity are reflecting the reality that Mary is not only the Jewish Mother of Jesus, but that she is the mother of each one of us. Because of this, she gladly assumes the appearance of every one of us. Similarly, Christ who is the savior of all nations visually belongs to no specific culture; rather, he avails himself to all.

What, then, to do with these exclusively Caucasian windows? Purists on one side of the spectrum would suggest that we must protect the stylistic purity of the building and ought not to add anything that is "foreign." Purists on the other side of the spectrum would question how anyone respectful of one's own ethnic tradition could worship in a building that is visually dominated by another ethnic tradition.

I would like to suggest that there is a middle road. Our Lady of La Vang very happily exists in the same building with Our Lady of Guadalupe, Our Lady of Africa, Our Lady of Tenderness, and Our Lady of the Immaculate Conception. Their simple testimony to the richness of our Catholic diversity ought to be an inspiration to us all.

Dear Johan,

I was quite disturbed last Sunday. For some inexplicable reason a group of African singers and dancers performed at our Mass. It does not seem reverent and it really took away the sacredness of the Mass. This is the United States, not the Congo.

Gentle Reader—

My studies at the "Belgian School of Diplomacy" come in handy at moments like this. It allows me to keep my cool and answer questions politely.

I suspect that your church was founded by and for European immigrants. And more than likely it was built using European architecture, European saints, European representations of Mary, Jesus, and Joseph, and so forth.

Today, however, our church is different, very different. We are not only Irish and Italian anymore. We are not only European anymore. Today we are European, African, Asian, Australian, American. Our liturgies are no longer segregated by nation. Rather we celebrate together as the one Body of Christ. Many Catholic communities throughout the United States represent the universality of the church and our liturgies do the same, or at least they ought to.

The essence of the Mass is, of course, the same, no matter where or by whom it is celebrated. However, the specifics of the celebration may differ quite a bit from country to country: architecture, music, vestments, dance, and so on. As we have become much more mobile and there is a great merging of cultures these different practices will and ought to meet in our liturgies. A Cameroon gospel procession, Aztec dances in honor of Our Lady of Guadalupe, Filipino songs, or Latin chant should not make us angry or distressed; rather, this great blend of cultures should lift our spirit since they testify to the universality and the rich diversity in our church.

A good measuring tool for the level of hospitality that characterizes your liturgies is whether all people who participate can recognize themselves in at least one aspect of the liturgy, be that a statue, a vestment, a song, or hopefully another person.

So please, pray for an openness of heart and mind and when you see Aztec dancers or hear conga drums in your church, rejoice and be glad, for the world church has come together to celebrate the mystery of God.

Dear Johan,

Someone corrected me, arguing that the Thanksgiving service was not "interdenominational" but "interfaith." Would you explain the difference? And while you are at it, are both allowed in the Catholic Church?

Gentle Reader—

The first part of your question is rather easy. An interfaith activity gathers people from different faith backgrounds, for example, Muslims, Hindus, Christians, Jews. The three great monotheistic religions among these are of course Judaism, Christianity, and Islam, which all trace their history back to the covenant between God and Abraham. As such Jews, Christians, and Muslims consider themselves to be children of Abraham.

An interdenominational activity is exclusively Christian as it brings together members of different Christian denominations— Episcopalians, Lutherans, Orthodox, Roman Catholics, Presbyterians, and the like.

Thus, an interdenominational service will be Christ-centered as it is celebrated by Christians. An interfaith service is a bit more complex as people from many different religions get together to pray according to their own traditions. With certain restrictions, both are allowed in the Catholic Church as a result of the groundbreaking work done by Vatican II.

Some of the most celebrated interfaith gatherings have happened in Assisi. These started in 1986 at the invitation of St. John Paul II, who invited representatives of all religions to come together to pray for peace. He repeated his invitation in 2002 and Pope Emeritus Benedict XVI extended the same invitation in 2011. In between the major gatherings in Assisi the Community of Sant' Egidio has organized an annual interfaith service for peace in the spirit of Assisi in a major city of the world.

To see leaders of different faiths come together to pray has been quite the contrast to the day-to-day violence that often happens between members of different faiths, most appallingly between Christians of different denominations and between the descendants of Abraham. It is only through shared prayer and ongoing dialogue that the much desired peace between nations will happen.

So, by all means, get together and pray. Prayer and dialogue with our sisters and brothers from different faiths is the only chance our war-torn world has at lasting peace.

Liturgical Furniture
and Objects

Dear Johan,

Last week I hosted some out of town guests. They asked why we did not have holy water "bowls" near the doors. I did not know. Do you?

Gentle Reader—

I would have been so tempted to ask them about the meaning of this gesture. Would they have made the connection with their baptism?

The act of blessing ourselves with holy water upon entering and leaving the church is intended as a reminder of our baptism and of the rights and obligations that come with that. Sadly, the small holy water stoops that serve this purpose are so far removed from the baptismal font in both size and amount of water that the connection is not readily made. On the contrary, dipping our fingers in those miniscule amounts of water and blessing ourselves is often done purely out of habit without much thought or impact. It is one of the things we do on our way from the profane into the sacred. Sometimes this reflexive action is questionably laden with a hint of pagan baggage.

The reason why we have these small stoops is due to the fact that previous to the Second Vatican Council, baptismal fonts were inaccessible. They were locked away in baptismal chapels and the water in them was hidden by metal covers. Thus, in lieu of the font, small holy water stoops were located at every door of the church, for easy access to holy water.

New and remodeled churches have large baptismal fonts at the entrance of the church. Their size and location make it clear that baptism is the first among the sacraments. In those churches, the font also functions as the place where people go to bless themselves upon entering and leaving the church. The only imaginable reason for preferring the stoops over the font must be habit and comfort, neither of which are acceptable.

Maybe you can invite your guests on their next visit to pass by the font when entering the church so they might remind themselves more effectively of their baptism. Would they not rather go to the source rather than to a minor tributary?

Dear Johan,

I attended a conference on liturgy and, to my great surprise (read: outrage), someone read Sacred Scripture from her handheld device during morning prayer. What do you make of this? Is this a new trend?

Gentle Reader—

These are interesting times. On the one hand, the monks of Saint John's Abbey in Collegeville, Minnesota, commissioned a handwritten and illuminated version of the Bible, something that had not been done in some five hundred years. The result is absolutely stunning. On the other hand, people have taken to proclaiming Scripture from their Kindles while others venerate icons on their iPads. The latter, of course, would have been unheard of some ten years ago and even today it seems shocking and inappropriate.

Like in most cases, a quick walk down memory lane is advised. It is good to remember that this is not the first time in Catholic history that the tangible presence of the Word in the liturgy has changed drastically. Think, for instance, of the beautiful handwritten *Exsultet* scrolls that were used during the Easter Vigil. These have now been retired to climate-controlled repositories.

Or consider the magnificently illuminated Evangeliaries or gospel books, which have joined the *Exsultet* scrolls in the vaults of our liturgical memories. All these, of course, over time have been replaced by the printed word. And even the printed word has gone through several iterations from hand-set letter printing, which still clearly testified to the impact of the human touch, to our completely computerized and automated printing today.

Your concern about the apparent next step in this trajectory is pertinent and appropriate. Will we soon raise a tablet during the gospel procession? I suspect and hope that for now we will hold on to the printed or, in some rare cases, the handwritten version of our gospel books.

Just to take it one step further, when asked about the veneration of icons on tablets, a Byzantine priest told me the following: "If these electronic images, not unlike prints of icons, encourage private devotion, great. Just keep them private and don't bring them into my church." Thus, I say, tablets are great tools that give us unlimited access to Scripture for our daily reading and research. Yet, as of today they have no place in the liturgical celebration.

Dear Johan,

Why don't we baptize in the baptismal font during the Easter Vigil? It is so beautiful and, not to forget, it is original to the building. More important, most of our community has been baptized in it.

Gentle Reader—

This is a topic after my heart as my dissertation was on baptismal fonts, both historic and new.

I am trying to imagine the situation in your church. I suspect that for the Easter Vigil some kind of temporary font is installed in the sanctuary to allow for full immersion of adults, rather than using the original font, which is undoubtedly smaller and located somewhere else in the church?

With the rediscovery of the importance of the sacraments of initiation—baptism, confirmation, and Eucharist—and the renewed emphasis on the fullness of the symbolic experience, baptismal praxis and architecture has undergone many changes in the past thirty years.

The most recent documents on the sacraments of initiation suggest that baptism by immersion, in the midst of the assembly, is the fuller mode of baptism. To do this with adults involves a lot of water. New baptismal fonts usually are created in such a way that they accommodate this praxis. Those who design today's baptisteries often look at the early churches for their inspiration.

On the other hand, older churches that have not been renovated often have but a small font, hidden in a back corner of the church. Infant baptisms sometimes continue to happen there, though these too should be celebrated in the midst of the assembly. For the Easter Vigil other accommodations are sometimes made for the full immersion of adults.

My suggestion to you is this: make a proposal to your pastor to bring your church up-to-date with the liturgical norms of today. Should you be concerned about losing the all-important original font, please be assured that there are great ways to incorporate that font in the new and larger font. That way, all your concerns will be alleviated and the liturgical norms will be more closely observed.

Dear Johan,

Most of the modern churches have one altar. Why does our church have so many and why do we only use the one in the sanctuary?

Gentle Reader—

Indeed, churches that are built or renovated after Vatican II only have one altar. It is the central eucharistic table, the locus of the sacramental presence of Christ, and a permanent symbol of Christ in our midst. It is reverenced with bows and kisses and incense.

The multiplicity of altars is the result of a combination of historical factors. First, since the early Middle Ages, a "high" theology of the Eucharist and of ordained ministry developed. Second, there was a great abundance of priests. Third, different groups such as guilds and confraternities desired to have an altar dedicated to their own salvation and, dare I say, glory. As a result, it was not uncommon for churches to have multiple altars at which different priests celebrated their own daily Mass for the intentions of the people who built and cared for the altars. And they would do it all at the same time.

The Second Vatican Council called some of this into question, returning the Catholic Church to an earlier and more authentic eucharistic theology and praxis. This included an emphasis on the active role of the assembly in the celebration of the Eucharist. The introduction of concelebration allowed priests to observe their own daily Mass obligation within the context of the assembly, rather than in solitude. And altars were no longer built for the personal or collective glory and salvation of an individual or a group.

Today, most churches have but one altar symbolizing the one who is Lord of all. The multiple altars you have in your church are theologically confusing and liturgically superfluous. Nevertheless, they may have artistic and historical importance. Because of that, they ought not to be shipped off to an architectural antiques shop but rather should be preserved and honored.

Dear Johan,

It seems like your church bells toll even when you don't have liturgy. Unlike other neighbors, I enjoy them but I would like to know why you ring them.

Gentle Reader—

Your keen sense of the acoustical landscape is to be commended. We do indeed ring them, even when we don't have liturgy. Beyond announcing services, church bells provide the acoustical décor for our churches. In a certain sense they are the voice of our churches.

While living in Belgium I used to delight in the glorious cacophony of church bells ringing almost the entire morning. When I moved to the United States I missed the sound of the bells. I thought the acoustical landscape the poorer for their absence.

Church bells are rung for different reasons. First and foremost, they are used to announce the liturgical life of the church. You will notice that before Sunday Eucharist, before weddings and funerals, the bells are rung. Each liturgy and each liturgical season has its own combination of bells, so as to allow the faithful to know which liturgy is going to take place. Did you know that church bells are completely silenced from the Gloria on Holy Thursday to the Gloria during the Easter Vigil?

Second, church bells are used to mark the times of the day. They do that in a twofold manner. On the one hand, they simply announce the time. Bells often toll on the hour and on the half hour. On the other hand, bells also mark prayer times. For centuries bells have invited people to a moment of private prayer in the morning, at noon, and in the evening. As the faithful heard the bells they would stop working, be they in the fields, in the factory, or at home, and everyone would pray the same prayer: the *Angelus*. The name for this prayer is derived from the Latin version of the traditional prayer said at that time, which begins as follows: *Angelus Domini nuntiavit Mariae* or "The angel of the

Lord declared unto Mary." It may be a romantic notion or a nostalgic longing, yet, it seems important that the church call people to stop at certain times of the day to focus on God.

Part of the prayer for the dedication of bells goes as follows: "May their voice direct our hearts toward you and prompt us to come gladly to this church" (Order for the Blessing of Bells, chap. 37 in *Book of Blessings*). So when you hear them, please join us in church or stop for a moment of private prayer.

Dear Johan,

I travel a lot yet I try to make Mass every Sunday. As a result I have visited many churches. Sometimes I am not sure if I am in a Catholic Church as I am unable to locate the tabernacle. Why is it not always located in the church proper?

Gentle Reader—

For those readers who might not know, the tabernacle is the receptacle in which the Blessed Sacrament is reserved so it may be used for Viaticum (Communion at the time of death), Communion of the sick, Communion outside of the celebration of the Eucharist, and adoration.

The word tabernacle is derived from the Latin *tabernaculum*, meaning tent or dwelling. It is used in the Bible in reference to God's dwelling place among the people or the people as the preferred dwelling place for God. As Christ is preeminently present in the Blessed Sacrament, it is only appropriate that the place in which the Blessed Sacrament is reserved is called a tabernacle.

The place and manner of reserving the Blessed Sacrament has changed substantially over time. Sometimes the Blessed Sacrament was reserved in the church, at other times in the sacristy. At some times the tabernacle was affixed, such as in the gothic Sacrament towers; and at other times the tabernacle was small and movable, such as the eucharistic dove suspended in the sanctuary or a small box placed near the altar.

At the end of the sixteenth century, in light of the Counter-Reformation, it became customary to place the tabernacle on most elaborate high altars. However, it was not until 1863 that all other manners of reservation were forbidden.

When traveling to European churches and museums, one will notice the rich diversity of the manner in which the Blessed Sacrament has been reserved over the years. In the United States, however, where the churches were built after the Counter-Reformation, there is no collective memory or archaeological repository of this diverse manner of reservation. Here, the obvious place for the tabernacle was on the high altar, that is, until the Second Vatican Council when a return to earlier liturgical praxis also occasioned a rethinking of the place for reserving the Blessed Sacrament.

Today's discipline is governed by the General Instruction of the Roman Missal (2011), which states, "In accordance with the structure of each church and legitimate local customs, the Most Blessed Sacrament should be reserved in a tabernacle in a part of the church that is truly noble, prominent, conspicuous, worthily decorated, and suitable for prayer" (314).

The document goes on to say that the tabernacle may be located either "in the sanctuary, apart from the altar of celebration, in an appropriate form and place, not excluding its being positioned on an old altar no longer used for celebration . . . or even in some chapel suitable for the private adoration and prayer of the faithful and organically connected to the church and readily noticeable by the Christian faithful" (315).

Thus there are different options when it comes to the location of the tabernacle. However, its location should be obvious to anyone visiting the church.

Dear Johan,

As I was walking through the sacristy I heard someone use the word *sacrarium*. I had never heard the word. I had to write it down so I could remember. Please tell me what it is.

Gentle Reader—

Wow, not very many people have this word as part of their vocabulary. Congratulations!

The root of the Latin word *sacrarium* is *sacer*, meaning sacred. Since ancient Roman times this word has been used to refer to a place where sacred objects are preserved. Roman temples, for example, had a sacrarium.

It is from *sacrarium* that the English words sacristy and sanctuary are derived. The sacristy is the place where liturgical vessels and vestments are preserved. It is also the place where liturgical ministers prepare themselves for the liturgy. The sanctuary is the area immediately surrounding the altar, often encompassing the ambo and the altar. In older churches, the sanctuary was architecturally delineated from the rest of the church. In more contemporary churches, the sanctuary is less clearly defined, hinting at the fact that the entire building is made sacred by sacred actions that are celebrated in it. As an aside, in some Christian traditions the word sanctuary is used to refer to the entire worship space.

The word sacrarium itself was adopted for liturgical use in English from the Latin for a very specific usage. A sacrarium is a sacred sink in the sacristy. This sink is not an ordinary sink as it cannot drain into the sewer system but rather needs to drain directly into the ground. This basin is exclusively intended for sacred usage.

The linens that are used during the liturgy are cleaned in the sacrarium. This includes the purificators or the linen napkins used to wipe the chalice during Communion and during the purification of the chalice. This also includes the corporal or the linen cloth, which is spread on the altar underneath the chalice and paten.

After the chalices have been purificated, meaning they have been rinsed with water that has been consumed, they can be further rinsed in the sacrarium. Consecrated wine is never to be poured down the sacrarium.

Finally, the sacrarium is also used for the proper disposal of blessed ashes, holy water, and oils.

Dear Johan,

Where have the consecration bells gone? I really miss them being rung at the time of the consecration. To me they demanded reverence.

Gentle Reader—

You wonder where the consecration bells have gone. I am more interested in where they have come from. So, you will get both.

As to your question, you can probably find them in religious attics and pious repositories since most of them have been retired for some fifty years. As to the latter, the answer is a bit more complicated. By the twelfth century the custom of receiving Communion by the faithful had mostly fallen out of practice. In its stead, a devotional gaze upon the consecrated host became increasingly important. This form of visual communion with the Body of Christ was thought almost as powerful as physical communion. And, one did not have to be in the state of grace to do so, which made it much easier.

To get the full effect of this answer you must remember that by the twelfth century the liturgy had been reduced to an exclusively clerical affair. People no longer understood what was going on since Latin was not their language. The rituals were conducted in sanctuaries that were far removed from sight and sometimes were completely hidden by curtains. The people themselves had resorted to all sorts of pious activities while the Mass was going on. All of this made it very difficult for the faithful to know when the consecration actually happened. As a result a number of practical rubrics were added to the Mass.

These rubrics included the ringing of the bell(s), which was intended to alert the people to the precise moment of the elevation so that all could stop their private prayers and communally gaze upon the consecrated host. It also included the custom of elevating the consecrated host so people might see, even from afar. In those places where curtains were used to hide the altar from ordinary people's sight, these were opened at the time of the elevation.

Since the Second Vatican Council, a greater emphasis has been placed on the active participation of the assembly in the celebration of the Eucharist so that alerting them to the important moment with a bell seems counterproductive. In addition, visual communion, thankfully, has been replaced again with the earlier practice of physical communion by the entire assembly through the reception of Holy Communion.

The current General Instruction of the Roman Missal allows the custom, when appropriate, for the server to ring the bell a little before the consecration so as to signal the faithful and again at the elevation. Nevertheless, I would suggest you just leave the bells where they have been for the past fifty-some years. Nostalgia is not an appropriate reason to resort to antiquated customs. And the use of sanctuary bells does not necessarily translate into a desired increase in devotion. Good liturgy and catechesis have proven to be much more effective.

Liturgical Posture
and Gestures

Dear Johan,

Can you tell me why some people hold hands during the Lord's Prayer and others don't? And is one better than the other?

Gentle Reader—

I too have noticed that some people hold hands, while others extend their hands or just fold their hands when praying the Lord's Prayer. None of these are explicitly forbidden and none of them are explicitly encouraged. And, as with most matters liturgical, this is a very touchy one, as people, not unlike myself, either hate or love the holding of hands during this important prayer.

We have a long history of liturgical gestures. The oldest prayer gesture is standing with outstretched arms. In Latin it is known as the *orans*, from the verb *orare*, to pray. Depictions of men and women in the orans position have been found among early Christian art. Today, the ordained ministers are the only ones explicitly instructed to engage in this ancient liturgical posture.

Wanting to underline the centrality of the Lord's Prayer with our bodies, we went in search of an appropriate posture. Rather than assume the one we relinquished centuries ago, we assumed another one, holding hands. But the two gestures are totally different. The orans is connected with the transcendental aspect of the prayer, the fact that the prayer is addressed to God; the holding of hands emphasizes the immanent aspect, the people's togetherness as they pray.

Of course, both emphases have their merit, yet, in pure sacramental theological thinking, the union of all Christians is primarily expressed by the sharing in the one Body and Blood of Christ, hence the term Communion (with the Body of Christ). The Lord's Prayer prepares us for this union as we stand together in orans (in prayer) before our Maker.

So, if I had to answer your question, which I suppose is the purpose of this book, I would suggest that you opt for the ancient gesture of the orans. In the same way as common language has been deemed unworthy of the liturgy so are common gestures. Holding hands seems just a bit too familiar.

Dear Johan,

Why do we need all the movement during liturgy? And I don't mean the procession. What I am talking about is the sitting, standing, kneeling . . . Wouldn't it be easier to just sit? All the movement is distracting.

Gentle Reader—

Your question brings us to the issue of bodily presence in the celebration of the liturgy. Our culture is somewhat schizophrenic when it comes to the body. We suffer from an obsession with the body while exhibiting a Victorian fear of the body. This, of course, impacts the way we see liturgy in relationship to our bodies.

When words fail us, our bodies take over as tears run down our cheeks or smiles brighten our faces. Though we fancy living above our eyebrows, we are essentially bodily creatures. This is why kneeling and standing, blessing oneself with holy water, bowing and genuflecting are part of the Roman Rite.

In addition, our bodies are both good learners and good teachers. Often one cannot help but wonder which came first, our faith in the presence of Christ in the Blessed Sacrament or our custom to make a sign of reverence when we enter a church. Do we believe because our bodies, through genuflecting and bowing, from childhood on, have taught us to believe? Or do we bow and genuflect because we were taught to believe? Probably a combination of both, yet, the power of the body as a learner and teacher should not be underestimated.

While certain words and gestures are reserved for the presider, at the same time he models for us how we are to be present at the Eucharist. When he stands, we stand; when he sits, we sit; when he bows, we bow. Other times during the liturgy we assume a posture different from that of the presider, which is befitting to our role in the assembly.

All these gestures weave a wonderful tapestry of bodily engagement of all of us in the celebration of the liturgy. After all, the liturgy is not merely an intellectual exercise celebrated above our eyebrows; rather the liturgy needs to be engaged in by the entire person, mind, body, and soul.

Dear Johan,

Why is it that people sign themselves with the sign of the cross on their foreheads, lips, and hearts before the reading of the gospel?

Gentle Reader—

Christians love to sign themselves and others with the sign of the cross. I remember asking my parents for a blessing every night before going to bed and they would sign my forehead with the sign of the cross. I sort of did it out of habit and yet deep down I realized it was important because I would not have dreamt of omitting this from our evening ritual, except maybe in a fit of rebellion during my teens. I will never forget asking my dad for his blessing during his last visit. It was his last blessing I ever received.

This custom of signing ourselves and others with the cross goes back to the early centuries of Christianity. Tertullian (ca. 160–ca. 220), for example, made reference to Christians wearing out their foreheads with the sign of the cross.

Every time we sign ourselves with the sign of the cross we place ourselves under the protection of the cross and we commit ourselves to Christ into whom we have been baptized.

Specific to your question, there is evidence that people signed themselves on the forehead and breast at the time of the gospel as early as the ninth century. By the eleventh century the signing at the time of the gospel also included the mouth.

Today's rubrics (prescriptions) for the celebration of the Eucharist as they are contained in the Roman Missal indicate that the person proclaiming the gospel is to say, "A reading from the holy Gospel according to . . ." Following that, he is to make the sign of the cross on the book, and then on his forehead, lips, and breast, "which everyone else does as well." The meaning of this gesture may be summarized as follows: May the word of the Lord guide our thoughts, our speech, and all our actions.

Dear Johan,

I don't think the practice of shaking hands during the sign of peace is particularly hygienic. I wish we would not have to do that.

Gentle Reader—

First off, if you are not comfortable doing this, then don't. No one will force you.

You make me think of the wonderful icon of Sts. Peter and Paul greeting one another with the kiss of peace. Although this is the original greeting between Christians, the church has wisely decided that some cultures might have a problem kissing strangers. So, other options have been provided: a hug, a handshake, or a bow. Each of these involves different levels of touching relative to the cultural comfort with physical contact.

The liturgy of the Roman Rite is celebrated in the midst of the reality and physicality of our human existence. As a result, much of what we do in our liturgies is physical: we submerge one another in water; we anoint with oil; we gather around the Easter fire; we wash feet and sometimes kiss them; we break bread and share it with one another; we drink from the one cup; we throw ashes at the beginning of Lent; we burn incense; we use candles, dripping with wax; we kneel and prostrate on the ground; we hug, touch, and kiss our books, our cross, the altar, and (sometimes) one another. We are the BODY of Christ. And our liturgy is profoundly messy. It is physical and sensuous. It cannot and should not be sanitized.

Your concern with hygiene, though, is real, very real. As an alternative to the customary ways of exchanging the sign of peace, you might consider touching the sleeved forearms of your Christian brothers and sisters or just wash your hands before and after the celebration of the Eucharist.

I noticed that some communities are anticipating your concern and have placed dispensers with disinfectant solutions throughout their church. This has given rise to a new liturgical procession as people walk to them following the sign of peace.

Dear Johan,

I attended Mass in a church where they had liturgical dance. It was very nice. Why can't we have it?

Gentle Reader—

I am reminded of an interview I saw many years ago. A reporter confronted Archbishop Marini, who was the papal master of ceremonies under Pope John Paul II, about the presence of Bangladeshi dancers at a papal Mass. The reporter reminded the archbishop that dancing during the liturgy was explicitly forbidden in the Western church. In response, Msgr. Marini stated that when the church gathers in Rome the world church gathers. I always have thought this answer brilliant and prophetic.

I wish I had more of a description of the church you attended and the kind of dance that happened there. As far as the rules go, they are indeed very clear. We can't have dance because it is simply not allowed, at least not in the church in the West. And when I think of the gentleman who insisted on having "dancing girls" at his funeral Mass, it is maybe for the best. Or is it?

I take comfort in the fact that the liturgy of the Roman Catholic Church is essentially kinetic, full of movements and gestures. The liturgy in itself, even without the addition of explicit dance, is already a very well-choreographed form of dance in its own right or rite. As a result, I have always wondered about the possibility of letting dance arise from the inside rather than impose dance on the liturgy from the outside. Just think of all the processions that are part of the liturgy: the entrance procession, gospel procession, procession with the gifts, communion procession, recessional. Why not enhance these processions from the inside out? The Dancing Church of Africa is the leader in this field.

And speaking of the African church, the world church that gathers in Rome according to Archbishop Marini is about to gather in many of our cities throughout the United States as many parishes become more and more diverse, integrating Catholics from all over the world. All of them bring their own experience of liturgy with them. Thus a parish in the West may very well comprise African dancers as well as Aztec dancers and the Bangladeshi sisters who danced at the above mentioned papal Mass.

If you don't have dance in your church yet, just be patient— the conch shell is about to be blown and the drumming is about to commence.

Dear Johan,

I was taught to genuflect before entering my pew in church. I am afraid not everyone does that anymore. Is that OK? Should I continue to genuflect?

Gentle Reader—

Sometimes we think that the liturgy begins with the opening song and procession. As a matter of fact, the liturgy begins much sooner than that. It begins when we get ready to make our way to church. From that moment on, we start transitioning from our daily world to the world of the liturgy. This process may involve getting ourselves and maybe our children ready. Then we make our way to church. We find a parking place, hopefully without much difficulty. We walk toward the church across a busy street or through a nicely landscaped garden. When we get to the doors of the church, the transition heightens. Pushing open the often heavy church doors, the wafts of incense and burning wax or the smell of evergreens or Easter lilies meets us.

At that moment we engage in two important transitional acts. First we make our way to the baptismal font, where we bless ourselves with holy water and remind ourselves of our baptismal rights and obligations. Then we proceed into the church proper and, before sitting or kneeling down in prayer, we genuflect as a sign of reverence toward the Blessed Sacrament, which is reserved in the tabernacle. In case the Blessed Sacrament is reserved in a separate chapel a profound bow toward the altar is appropriate as the altar is a symbol of Christ. Both are threshold gestures. They complete the transition from our daily life to our liturgical life, not that the one ever ignores the other.

These transitional gestures are extremely important. They express what we believe and they reinforce those beliefs. The loss of these gestures is not only a sign of the loss of reverence due the Blessed Sacrament; it will also compound that loss of reverence.

So to answer your question, please continue genuflecting and maybe add a visit to the baptismal font. Hopefully your great example will encourage others to follow suit.

Dear Johan,

Why do we wash feet on Holy Thursday? I used to worship in a parish where we washed hands. That seems much more hygienic.

Gentle Reader—

Let me tell you a story. One Holy Thursday, long ago, I celebrated the Sacred Triduum at the motherhouse of a religious community. Before the service of the Lord's Supper, I watched several elderly sisters being brought into the chapel. Their wheelchairs were lined up around the altar. Others came in using their walkers. Still others walked on the arm of another sister or a nurse. The service was simple, yet very beautiful. At the time of the footwashing, the priest suggested that we were going to wash one another's feet. As a liturgical purist, I was simply mortified at the thought. What could this mean? Why were we straying from the custom of the priest washing the feet of twelve men, symbolizing Christ washing the feet of the apostles?

I swallowed my liturgical pride and tried to enter into the experience. As I was pondering all this, I noticed a sister being helped to the front of the chapel. When she arrived at the row of wheelchairs, she was helped to her knees in front of one of her sisters. Gently and with great difficulty, she took the slippers off her sister's feet. A bowl with water was brought to them. She placed her sister's feet in the water and tenderly washed them. Then she dried them and kissed them. I felt tears running down my cheeks.

These feet, which had walked in the service of the church for more than seventy years, were tenderly washed by these hands, which had served the church for more than sixty years. In that moment I finally got why Jesus told us to wash one another's feet. It is all about bending down in humility to serve one another.

The washing of the feet is not a superfluous ritual gesture or a simple reenactment of what Jesus did two thousand years ago. Rather it is an efficacious ritual rehearsal of what all of us are called to do every day of our life. That's why we wash feet on Holy Thursday. You will not get this from washing hands. And by the way, there is nothing hygienic about the Gospel as it is all about getting dirty with those who are dirty.

Dear Johan,

When I was a child, priests would wash their hands during the Mass. Then they stopped, and now they are doing this again. What is up with that?

Gentle Reader—

The obvious question here is about the washing of the hands. There also seems to be a subtext pertaining to changes in the liturgy. Let me first speak to the latter. As you know, the liturgy is an evolving reality. Just think of how the Tridentine Mass differed from the Last Supper and how today's celebration of the Eucharist differs from the Tridentine Mass. Of course, the essence has always been the same, but the rituals continue to evolve and they differ from place to place. Sometimes, I think all of us suffer from liturgical provincialism: the way in which the liturgy is celebrated in our parish is the way in which it is done (read: ought to be done) all around the world. Please be assured that the liturgy has changed a lot since the Last Supper and will continue to do so.

Now, back to the *lavabo* or the washing of hands by the priest. As is the case with many rituals, the origin of the *lavabo* is very practical and its continued use became purely symbolic. Just imagine the offertory procession in the early church and in the Middle Ages. This was not a stylized procession with bread and wine and monetary gifts. On the contrary, people brought the fruits of the land to be offered to God for the well-being of the community. After receiving these and incensing them, it was necessary for the priest to wash his hands. Once the procession of the gifts became stylized and the hand washing became a symbolic act, its meaning shifted from literal dirt to spiritual dirt. The priest prays, "Wash me, O Lord, from my iniquity / and cleanse me from my sin" when washing his hands.

Today, in an age of heightened hygienic concern, the *lavabo* seems to serve both a spiritual and a practical purpose: a cleansing of literal and spiritual dirt, both at the same time. I am waiting for the moment when a small pump containing antibacterial gel will be brought to the priest and ceremoniously pumped into his hands. Oh wait, I am sure it already happens somewhere. I wonder what liturgists will write about this fifty years from now?

Dear Johan,

Why does the priest drop a particle of the host in the wine at Communion time?

Gentle Reader—

This is a great example of how a ritual act can be introduced into the liturgy on the basis of a specific theology, how the act is retained in the liturgy even after having lost its original meaning, and how a new theology is attached to this ritual.

The specific ritual act you mention goes back to the early church. The bishop, as the successor of the apostles, was the one who presided over the community and over the celebration of the Eucharist, its primary symbol of unity. As Christianity spread throughout the Roman Empire, particularly outside of the cities, it became necessary for the bishops to send some of their priests into the country. These priests represented the bishop to the community and they presided over the celebration of the Eucharist on Sunday. As a symbol of ecclesiastical communion and unity, the bishop sent a part of the eucharistic bread that was consecrated at his Mass to the parishes in the hinterlands. The local priests would add this particle to the cup. This particle was called the *fermentum* or yeast.

Today, this particle no longer comes to us from the Eucharist celebrated by the bishop, although the theological memory and symbolic meaning still are residually present. It is now called the "commingling" and it primarily symbolizes the unity of the Body and Blood of Christ. It also symbolizes our sharing in the Body of Christ.

Liturgical Praxis

Dear Johan,

I attended a Lutheran synod assembly hosted by a Catholic church. They sing so well. Why is it that Catholics don't sing as much?

Gentle Reader–

Many years ago, I told a friend how I appreciated the way he sang wholeheartedly during the liturgy. He smiled and shyly thanked me. I then told him I hoped the next step would be for him to sing correctly. The look on his face made me want to cry.

Hosting a Lutheran synod assembly was a marvelous thing to do. Not only was it great ecumenical outreach, it also seems to have called Catholics who were in attendance to ponder their singing, or the lack thereof. If it was anything like a similar Lutheran liturgical experience I once had, it must have been a service unlike any other. I imagine the windows were vibrating with sound. The level of participation of the congregation probably met the expectations set out by the Second Vatican Council. How remarkable that Lutherans show us how to fulfill the vision of this great Catholic council.

Your question as to our lack of musical participation on Sundays is one that plagues my mind and weighs heavy on my heart. Surely, many of us have all sorts of reasons to justify our lack of singing: the music is too difficult, too fast, too high, too low, too slow, too . . . "If only you would choose music we know . . ." I have heard them all.

I am afraid that much of this is nothing but an attempt at reasoning ourselves out of our responsibility to participate in the singing. We really need to enhance our culture of liturgical participation. We need to embrace the fact that we are called to sing. We need to realize that without our voice the liturgy is less. We need to believe that the choir is not the primary music maker, but that we are.

I regret the words to my friend, many years ago. I wish I could tell him that I now realize that the most important thing is to sing with your heart, your voice will follow. So let us sing the liturgy together so that we too can make the windows of our hearts vibrate with joyful sound.

Dear Johan,

Why don't you provide a printed version of the Sunday readings? They do this in many other churches and it makes things so much easier.

Gentle Reader—

What we are after in the liturgy is not ease, rather sacramentality and efficacy. Let me explain.

I, too, have celebrated the liturgy in churches that provide the readings in printed form. Inevitably, the announcement of the reading causes people to bury their heads and their attention into their text as they communally tune out the lector. In this case, the proclamation of the Scriptures has effectively been replaced with a collective reading. In a sense the liturgical celebration has ceased in favor of some kind of collective Bible study.

Though Bible study is a worthy and necessary endeavor, it differs greatly from the celebration of the Liturgy of the Word. In essence, the liturgical celebration is sacramental while Bible study is not. The sacramental nature of the liturgy is relative to Christ's presence in it. When it comes to the Eucharist we believe that Christ is present in the celebrating assembly, in the presiding priest, in the Word that is proclaimed and received, and above all in the eucharistic species.

The sacramentality or the presence of Christ in the Word is based on the fact that the Word is proclaimed in the midst of an assembly that is ready to receive the Word. In other words, it is the proclamation and the reception that make the Word sacramental. Collective silent reading does not.

Furthermore, the proclamation of the Word is not merely the reading of a story, either individually or even communally. It is so much more than that. The word of God proclaimed during our liturgies is the same Word by which all that exists was created at the dawn of time. That same powerful and creative word of God is operative during the Liturgy of the Word. And even when, God forbid, we tune out because "we have heard the story before," the spoken word of God is creatively at work in our mind, heart, and soul.

In an attempt to visualize how this works, I often think of the word of God proclaimed in our midst as the hands of God and the listening assembly as the clay. Week after week, as we listen to the Word, God's hands mold us more and more into the image of Christ. Another image is that of a rock in a riverbed. The word of God is the water and we are the rock. Like the water polishes the rock, the word of God polishes us to become better Christians.

The only acceptable reasons for printing the readings in the booklet are first, to assist people with hearing disabilities; second, to compensate for a faulty sound system; third, to assist people in their meditation on the readings either before or after the liturgy.

So when the lector announces the reading, rather than wishing you had a printed text, please give your full attention to the proclamation of God's word. Let the Word wash over you, let the Word mold you so that after a lifetime of listening to the word of God you will have become the Word you heard and received.

Dear Johan,

I notice that in other churches the liturgy does not last more than fifty minutes. We take much longer. I'm not complaining; I am just curious. Why do we need more time to celebrate the same liturgy?

Gentle Reader—

Your question reminds me of a failed dinner several years ago. We were on our way to a concert and decided to have dinner on the way there. As we were somewhat in a hurry, I asked the server how long it would take before the meal arrived. He looked at me indignantly and wondered aloud if I might be confusing fine dining with fast food. He also suggested the names of a couple restaurants down the road that might better suit our needs. We made a quick exit and I have never been back.

What has happened to us? And what has happened to the way we eat? When was the last time you sat down for a leisurely dinner, prepared from scratch? That is what we did every day when I was growing up. Things have changed so much in our rapid-paced, quick-bite, and fast-serve society. As a result, fine dining has become an endangered activity. And I am afraid that fine liturgies will follow suit.

As is the case with fine dining, there is nothing quick or fast about the Eucharist, which rehearses us for the heavenly banquet. I feel fortunate to be part of a church community where people believe in celebrating the liturgy to its fullest. That means that we take our time, singing, praying, praising God for the marvelous deeds accomplished in Jesus Christ.

If indeed the liturgy is the "source and summit" of everything a Christian community does, as the Second Vatican Council states, then we need to take that to heart. Limiting this to fifty minutes or less seems a bit stingy!

When asked how long any given liturgy will last, I try to re-frain from telling people that they are confusing fine liturgy with fast liturgy and that they might be better served in a church down the road. Rather, I smile and answer that it will last as long as it needs to last.

Dear Johan,

I am always struck by the stern look on people's faces when they are at church, especially when they return from Communion. Where is the joy of Christianity?

Gentle Reader—

Ghanaian Cardinal Peter Turkson, the president of the Pontifical Council for Justice and Peace, tackled that very question when asked about the state of the liturgy. In response he expressed his surprise that in the West, the same people who exhibit great passion and burst with excitement during sporting events show little to no emotion during the celebration of the Eucharist. Though they have no problem singing at football games, he continued, they seem to experience the singing of hymns in church as a true penitential exercise. By contrast, he said, people in the African churches sing with gusto and on occasion add some movement to express their joy at hearing the Good News.

Having just attended a baseball game, I can testify to the exuberance with which supporters cheer their team. This, indeed, contrasts starkly with the blank faces and sealed lips of many people during the celebration of the Eucharist. They seem as happy to be in church as they might be while at the dentist for a root canal.

The reality is that Christians have responded in varied ways to the mystery of salvation. For some this is a very serious matter that ought to be pondered. For others this is a joyous reality that must be celebrated. This response is often related to the societal, cultural, and ethnic characteristics of individuals and communities. When our churches were more homogenous, no one was surprised by a neighbor's reaction. Today, with the ever increasing diversity in our churches, some people prefer sober expressions, others will be more exuberant. All of these are valid expressions. All of these add color to the liturgy.

In those communities that still largely suffer under "northern exposure," solemn containment will be the premier mode of liturgical behavior. However, even those communities ought to remember the difference between solemn containment and a frown. The fact is that we have been saved and that is something to be exuberantly celebrated, not quietly endured.

Dear Johan,

I have noticed that people in other Catholic churches, even in this country, do things differently. That concerns me. Why do they have the need to change things? Aren't there any rules that would ensure this?

Gentle Reader—

Am I wrong to think that you wish everyone would celebrate the way you celebrate the liturgy in your church? If so, you might suffer from a condition that is called liturgical provincialism. The only known cure is to celebrate the liturgy often and in many different parishes.

One of the great myths that plague our church is that we ought to strive for uniformity in our liturgical celebration. Some might even be tempted to suggest that there should be uniformity in all we do. Not only is this said to be better, it is also suggested that this is how it has always been. I am afraid this kind of thinking is erroneous on both accounts because it is neither historically accurate nor have attempts at imposing uniformity proven to be better for the church.

It seems like I say this over and over again but diversity is not only an essential characteristic of Catholic liturgy but it is also greatly beneficial. And what is shocking to many, change has always been par for the course. Naturally, the essence of the liturgy has been retained at any given time and in any given place.

After Jesus told his disciples to "do this in memory of me" they set out to do so. Except the "this" took slightly different forms depending on where and when this mandate was honored. Isn't it amazing that the first papal attempt at unifying the celebration of the Eucharist was not until 1277, when Pope Nicholas III ordered that the Missal (or the book containing all the texts for the Eucharist) that was used at the papal court was to be used throughout the Diocese of Rome? This Missal also gradually spread throughout Europe, but individual bishops were free to adapt the Missal for their own use.

In response to the Protestant Reformation, the Council of Trent desired to more clearly define Catholicism, especially Catholic liturgy. As a result they declared that the Roman Rite, or the liturgy as it was celebrated in the Diocese of Rome, was to be used in all Catholic churches throughout the world. Exception was granted to those churches using missals reflecting other venerable rites, such as the Milanese Rite, which originated in Milan, and the Gallican Rite, which was celebrated throughout Gaul.

In 1570 Pope Pius V promulgated a new Roman Missal for universal use. That Missal, though amended numerous times by successive popes, remained in effect until the Roman Missal of Pope Paul VI of 1969, which made substantial changes to the Catholic liturgy, not in the least by promoting its celebration in the vernacular.

Even today, as we celebrate according to the most recent version of the Roman Rite dating back to 2011, both uniformity and diversity characterize our celebrations. We do, of course, have prescribed texts, movements, and gestures. However, the rubrics cannot contain the living liturgy, which is not celebrated in a vacuum but by people of flesh and blood in a specific place and time. Thus, every community, relative to its own ethos, will celebrate the same liturgy in a slightly different way.

So, in response to your suggestion that it would be nice if everybody celebrated exactly in the same manner, I must simply say that it would not. Not only would requiring absolute uniformity be impossible but it would also be detrimental to the very essence of the living liturgy itself.

Dear Johan,

I was very annoyed that someone's cell phone went off during Easter services. Worse, the person sitting next to me was texting throughout the service. What is going on?

Gentle Reader—

You allude to two annoyances. First, the fact that people leave their phones on. Second, that people use their handheld devices.

In response to the first I would like to sheepishly suggest that this might be an honest mistake. One time I forgot to turn off my phone while I was presiding at morning prayer. We were all gathered in our weekday chapel and I was in the midst of the closing collect, my hands lifted in prayer, as the phone in my pocket started to ring. I think I have never been more embarrassed. It did not help when I realized that it was our receptionist who was trying to reach me. This experience cured me forever from keeping my phone on when doing something important. Nevertheless, you have a good point. People should turn off all handheld devices during the celebration of the liturgy.

In response to your second annoyance, I am afraid that this one is much more difficult to deal with as it is something that pervades our culture today. Last week I enjoyed dinner at a lovely restaurant with some good friends. I was struck by the number of times my friends checked their handheld devices. Sometimes they did this in the open, other times conspicuously holding their devices in their laps. Through it all they pretended to continue the conversation and to enjoy the food. I felt cheated. When questioned they answered that they like to multitask. I reminded my friends that I am a jealous friend who does not believe in multitasking when it comes to friendship.

More important and in response to your question, I do not believe in multitasking when it comes to worshiping our God. So, when you come to church, forget about multitasking, rather concentrate and give worship where worship is due and that does not include your handheld device. And should the priest have a brilliant message you are dying to share with your friends, please be patient. Even when sent after the end of the liturgy your five thousand Facebook friends will be appreciative.

Dear Johan,

Why is it that so many people leave church before the end of Mass? I am saddened to see people leave as soon as they receive Communion.

Gentle Reader—

Last week, as I was trying to sing the closing hymn, people around me were putting on their coats and obviously were waiting for me to let them out of the pew. Not only did they not stay till the end, but they made it impossible for me to pay attention till the end. What difference do a few minutes make? Unless they had a soufflé waiting in the oven, I saw no reason for their hurry.

I have always been annoyed by this. When I was a teenager my aunt found me making a sign saying "leaving already?" My plan was to wait outside church with the sign so early departees would be shamed by my sign. Thankfully, my wise aunt talked me out of it.

Since those days I have softened quite a bit. So, I am not for harsh words or placing liturgical watchdogs at all doors, but I must admit that I am disheartened by the so-called "post-communion exodus." How come people don't want to spend some quiet time after receiving Communion? This is not a liturgical drive-through.

The liturgical patience of those who stay after receiving Communion is often tested by the endless announcements after Communion. Who can blame them? Even I am tested by those. But I persevere, why can't others?

What saddens me most, though, is that our liturgical assembly seems fractured when people start leaving. It is a bit like people leaving early at a dinner party. That does not speak well of the party. I would feel horrible as the host. I feel horrible as a fellow guest.

I suspect the only thing we can do is make the liturgy as beautiful as we can so people will want to stay. And after that, it is really out of our hands.

Dear Johan,

Sometimes we say the Nicene Creed after the intercessions, and sometimes we don't. Isn't it a part of the Mass? What gives?

Gentle Reader—

I hope we never say the Creed after the intercessions. That would be a rubrical mishap. The Creed is to follow the homily and precede the intercessions. On a rare occasion the rubrical mishap we make may be that of omission. Mind you, the liturgy police is always quick to point this out.

And, indeed, the Creed is part of the Sunday Eucharist. It is good to remember, though, that besides the Nicene Creed there are two other forms we can use, namely, the Apostles' Creed and the Baptismal Creed.

People are undoubtedly most familiar with the Nicene Creed as it is the most widely used. It is called the Nicene Creed after the location of the first ecumenical council, which was held in Nicea in 325. The original form of this Creed was adopted there. The current form, which is an expansion of the original Creed, is said to have been adopted at the Council of Constantinople in 381. Because of this the full name of the Nicene Creed is the Nicene-Constantinopolitan Creed.

The shorter yet less known Apostles' Creed is said to have originated in the second century. The first written testimony to its existence, though, is much more recent as it is mentioned in a letter written by Ambrose of Milan to Pope Siricius in 390. The earliest complete text we have of this Creed is no older than the beginning of the eighth century. The Roman Missal indicates that this Creed may be used instead of the Nicene Creed, especially during Lent and Easter. This undoubtedly has to do with the reference in this Creed to Jesus' descent into hell.

The third option, which is only used for the Easter celebrations as well as for baptism and confirmation, is the Baptismal Creed. Its form differs from the other two in that this Creed is done in a question-and-answer format.

Regardless of what Creed is chosen, the Creed is the assembly's response to the readings and the homily as well as the affirmation of the community's shared faith in preparation for the prayers of the faithful. It should not be omitted; better yet, if possible it should be sung.

Dear Johan,

I hear you speak about active participation in the liturgy all the time. Though I know it's important, sometimes I just don't feel like it.

Gentle Reader—

In his encyclical *Mediator Dei* (1947) Pope Pius XII called for a revision of the liturgy with greater and deeper participation of the laity in mind. The Tridentine liturgy, which was used at that time, was mostly inaccessible to the people. The priest, with his back to the people, recited the Mass in Latin and relied on servers for the responses. The people in the pew, on the other side of the communion rail, were left to their own devices. Unable to understand a word of what was sung or said, they prayed the rosary, read devotional books, and maybe listened to a sermon that was delivered almost independently from the Mass. At the time of the consecration the *Sanctus* bell drew their attention to the altar for ocular or visual communion as hardly anyone received Communion at Sunday Eucharist.

    Sacrosanctum Concilium (1963), the Constitution on the Sacred Liturgy promulgated in light of the Second Vatican Council, picked up on the call by Pius XII and made one of the principle goals of the liturgy the full, active, and conscious participation of all. As a result, the liturgy was to be celebrated in the vernacular, the priest was to face the people, and the liturgy was simplified and streamlined.

In the past fifty years we have made great progress in implementing what the council envisioned. There have been some difficult moments and maybe some setbacks, but all in all the vision of the council is being realized.

The point you make is a very good one, though. First, the goal of the council was to make the liturgy accessible to all, that is, celebrate the liturgy in such a way that everyone who attends can understand and participate in the liturgy. This is a mandate placed on the liturgy and not placed on you. Second, the council in no way is forcing anyone to participate by singing or standing or responding or kneeling. These are all suggestions that anyone moved by the liturgy will hopefully engage in, but sometimes, as you say, we simply cannot.

There are those moments when the weight of the world is too heavy for any one of us to shoulder. I remember how I felt when my father died. After I received the unexpected news I did the only thing I knew to do: I participated in the celebration of the Eucharist. However, I could not bring myself to sing. There was no way I could respond without breaking down. I did not even have the strength to stand or kneel. So I sat in the back of the church and let the liturgy wash over me. Better yet, I let the liturgy lift me up. I did not sing, but the voices of my sisters and brothers in Christ sang for me. I did not respond, but the assembly responded for me. I did not participate in any of the movements, but the Body of Christ did that for me.

Sometimes, being there is the only level of participation we can engage in and sometimes that is enough, because we can rely on the rest of the Body of Christ to do the work of the liturgy. It is the hope that in those moments our interior participation is effectively aided by the community's exterior participation.

Dear Johan,

I have noticed that there is much more talking in the back of the church before Mass and even during Mass than there used to be. Don't these people get it?

Gentle Reader—

You are quite correct, things have changed. Far gone are the days when we did not dare to even whisper after we had entered church. Today, many people enter a church in the same manner as they might enter a restaurant or bar. And worse, they continue their chatter even after the liturgy has begun.

Of course, there is something really beautiful about the joy people express upon seeing fellow Christians when entering church. They shake hands, hug, and kiss. New babies are crooned over while visiting college students receive jovial slaps on the back.

I also marvel at the people who engage in their pious routine after quietly slipping past all the hubbub. They walk to the baptismal font where they pause briefly to intentionally bless and remember their baptismal commitment. From there they go to one of the shrines to light a candle. Finally, they make their way to a pew. They genuflect, enter the pew, and kneel down in quiet prayer. All of this is done in perfect silence somewhat hassled by the friendly banter all around them.

Though both are valid, at times the sounds of enthusiasm and the silence of prayer collide. In order for both to coexist, contemporary churches often have a gathering space where arriving parishioners can meet and greet. They also have a Blessed Sacrament chapel where silence and reverence prevail.

Many older churches have neither a gathering space nor a Blessed Sacrament chapel. This requires churchgoers to exercise liturgical patience and to honor the spiritual needs of others. Those who are more inclined to visit ought to make sure they control their decibels of enthusiasm and end their socializing before the liturgy begins. Those who prefer quiet prayer over joyous encounters are at a disadvantage as their silence is often drowned out. My advice to them is to pray for ever deepening patience as well as for the needs of those people who annoy them with their enthusiasm.

Dear Johan,

My father recently passed away after a long struggle with cancer. During the last weeks of his life we selected the readings and the music for his funeral. He also asked me to do a eulogy. When the time came my father's priest changed everything and did not allow a eulogy. I feel like I betrayed my father.

Gentle Reader—

Allow me first and foremost to assure you that you did not betray your father. You tried to follow his wishes and circumstances made it impossible for you to honor them. It was not for your lack of trying.

By contrast to the times when the funeral liturgy was pretty much set and no decisions had to be made, today the church invites members of the family and friends to assist in the preparation of the liturgy. This is a wonderful opportunity for the family to select readings and music that fit their spiritual needs as we prepare to pray for their deceased relative as well as for the survivors.

The best way to do this is in consultation with your parish priest. This avoids unfortunate situations when the family's hopes and expectations for the service are crushed because they are some-times ill-informed and occasionally cannot be accommodated.

The greatest disconnect is that the survivors want the service to be about the deceased. That, of course, is also the wish of the church, however, within the context of faith. Above all, the church approaches the deceased as a member of the Body of Christ. Survivors often have a more individualistic approach. They don't easily understand that the fact, for example, that the deceased loved to fish does not make his tackle box or fishing pole a liturgically appropriate symbol. Or the fact that she was a very independent person does not make Frank Sinatra's *My Way* suitable as a communion meditation.

Pertaining to eulogies the church is very clear that they are forbidden, though "words of remembrance" are allowed. The distinction between the two is that eulogies essentially are words of praise. The word eulogy itself implies this as it comes from the Greek for *speaking well* about someone. Words of remembrance, on the other hand, implies an honest speech about the deceased person, covering both gifts and faults. These can be offered by a member of the family or a friend prior to the final commendation.

Now, even though the church makes allowance for this, local dioceses may caution against them for a number of reasons. First, they can really run out of hand, both in length as in content. And once a person starts to speak, it is difficult to elegantly make him or her stop. Second, this speech tends to interrupt the flow of the liturgy. Third, since this happens during the liturgy, the appearance may be given that what is said is church sanctioned or at least has been approved by the pastor. Because of this pastors are cautious when a request for a eulogy is made and sometimes forbid them altogether.

Though eulogies, certain songs, and mementos may not be suitable for the funeral liturgy, these can be accommodated at other times, for example, during the visitation the night before or even during the lunch following the funeral. The added advantage is that these settings are less formal and less intimidating.

Though things did not turn out completely as your dad wished, preparing his funeral together was a great gift to him, to yourself, and to all survivors. Unlike other families, you did not have to wonder what your dad would have loved. I wish more people would prepare their own funeral. Just one caveat, it is best done in conversation with the pastor so as to avoid the kind of unpleasant experience you encountered.

Liturgical Theology

Dear Johan,

Liturgy is taken very seriously in our church. We enjoy it very much, but there are times when I wonder about the purpose of it all. Any thoughts?

Gentle Reader—

Even those of us who are immersed in the liturgy are occasionally tempted by this question: What's it all for? So, don't despair.

In a way, our liturgical mandate is summed up in the Second Vatican Council's document on the liturgy, which identifies liturgy as the "source and summit" of the Christian life. It is with baptism/confirmation that our life as Christians begins and with the rite of Christian burial that we are accompanied to our grave. We journey from baptism to burial nourished by the Eucharist, ordered by holy matrimony or holy orders, and healed by the sacrament of reconciliation and the sacrament of the sick.

Moreover, in these liturgies we celebrate during our earthly journey we are rehearsed in how we can be more like Christ, thus contributing to the Body of Christ. To this end, the liturgy both soothes and challenges us. The liturgy reaches out to people in their specific life situation to nourish, encourage, and heal. The liturgy also is intended to stretch our horizons and to pull us out of our small and self-centered worlds.

The ultimate test of a Christian community's liturgical life is whether it changes lives. Does our liturgy call us to be one with the poor, to share our table with the hungry, to visit the sick, to embrace the dying? If so, then we are well on our way to being more like Christ and our liturgy, no matter its style, is truly a foretaste and a rehearsal of the eternal Jerusalem.

In the end, if the liturgy does not change us into becoming more like Christ, then it is nothing but ritual fits and follies. So, let's celebrate the liturgy well so it may change our hearts and minds and send us into the world to make a difference.

Dear Johan,

I have not gone to confession since I was in grade school. I would like to start going on a regular basis but I am a little intimidated since I don't remember what I am supposed to do. How can I relearn this important sacrament?

Gentle Reader—

The sacrament of reconciliation, formerly known as confession, is probably one of the most unknown, undervalued, and underestimated sacraments we have. The *Catechism of the Catholic Church* now groups the seven sacraments into the sacraments of initiation (baptism, confirmation, Eucharist), the sacraments of healing (reconciliation, anointing of the sick), and the sacraments at the service of the communion (holy orders and matrimony).

In its discussion of the sacrament of reconciliation, the Catechism suggests five different names for the same sacrament: conversion, confession, penance, forgiveness, reconciliation. In a way, these five names refer to the different stages a person goes through when preparing for and celebrating the sacrament.

- First, we need to realize that certain thoughts and actions are harmful to ourselves and the community and thus harm our relationship with God.

- Second, we name our sins before God, in the presence of a priest.

- Third, we express our willingness to repent for the sins committed and to do penance to make amends.

- Fourth, God heals us from our sins through the absolution spoken by the priest.

- Fifth, true conversion, confession, and penance lead to forgiveness and reconciliation with ourselves, with the church, and with God.

Ordinarily, this sacrament is celebrated privately between the confessor and the person making his or her confession. The rite is very simple: after the sign of the cross and the greeting, the priest proclaims a brief passage from Scripture. After this, the penitent confesses his or her sins to the priest. In response, the priest may give advice and suggest some form of satisfaction, which most often consists of prayer, fasting, or giving of alms. Then, the penitent prays for forgiveness. The priest absolves the penitent from his or her sins and together they give praise to God.

I suggest you make an appointment with your priest and schedule your next confession. Do let him know it has been a while. I am sure he will be happy to navigate you through the sacrament. Also, most parishes have prayer cards available in their reconciliation chapels so you need not worry about knowing those by heart.

Dear Johan,

My friends tell me that because the Bible is the word of God, we have to believe it all. Is that true? If so, how can that be?

Gentle Reader—

As you know, when we read from the Bible in a liturgical setting, we end the proclamation with "The word of the Lord" or "The Gospel of the Lord." This is an affirmation that we indeed believe the Word proclaimed to be the word of God. Does that mean that God wrote every single word of the Bible down or maybe dictated the Bible to a human scribe? We can be pretty sure that he did not.

As Catholics we honor the Bible as the word of God for two reasons. First, it tells the story of the relationship between God and the people from the time of creation to the time of salvation with all its ups and downs and all its human progress and setbacks. The Bible, then, is first of all the book that narrates not as much the history but more so the relationship between God and the people and the people's experience of God speaking to them in many different situations.

Second, the Bible is considered the word of God because its very existence is divinely inspired. As such the Bible contains God's word conceived in human language, written by and for specific people but with a deep meaning for all generations since.

What, then, about those people who insist that since the Bible is the word of God, we should interpret it literally? Even if we thought we should, certain biblical passages literally prevent us from doing so. I suggest that you and your friends read the Bible cover to cover and try to insist on its literal interpretation. You might be surprised, if not shocked, by the things you would find yourselves doing if interpreting the text literally. Theoretically, of course, the literal interpretation seems to be a more respectful approach to the word of God. In reality, it is not.

Thankfully, God's intent for the Bible is spiritual, rather than literal. Thus, a spiritual interpretation of the Bible is even better than a literal interpretation. In order to do that, we need to know the context in which each passage has been written. This is not always easy. That is why homilies are of the utmost importance.

They are intended to break open the Word that was just proclaimed and to assure that we understand what God's plan is for us, today.

I don't suspect this will convince your friend. However, I do hope it confirmed you in your beliefs.

Dear Johan,

I am alarmed by the conservative trends in the liturgy today. The changes in the celebration of the Eucharist that were recently imposed on us are but the tip of the iceberg. What should I do?

Gentle Reader—

I sometimes wish Jesus had left us with much clearer directives as to the celebration of the Eucharist. Of course, he didn't and undoubtedly purposefully so. Nevertheless, I wonder what exactly he had in mind when he told us, "do this in memory of me"?

Much has changed in the liturgy since Jesus gathered with his followers to break the bread and share the wine on the night before he died. The liturgy has evolved together with the church as it became more and more complex. Some of the landmark events that changed the liturgy over the course of time are the unification of the liturgy of the early Christian churches into the Roman Rite, the codification of the liturgy in light of the Council of Trent, and the fundamental changes in the liturgy after the Second Vatican Council.

Today's liturgy is characterized by the following five affirmations:

- The Eucharist is the source and summit of everything we do as a community.

- The entire Body of Christ in its varied ministries celebrates the liturgy.
- Everyone is called to full, conscious, and active participation in the liturgy.
- Christ is present in the gathered assembly, the celebrant, the Word proclaimed, and above all the consecrated bread and wine.
- The Body of Christ worships best when using the local language and honoring local customs.

These fundamental theological concepts were published over fifty years ago in a groundbreaking document: the Constitution on the Sacred Liturgy (1963). On the basis of this document the liturgy was revised. The first edition of the revised liturgy was published in the Roman Missal of 1969. In the year 2000 the fifth revision of this instruction was promulgated in Latin. As in every round of revisions, there are some clarifications and some adaptation in light of contemporary liturgical needs. We have been using this version of the liturgy since Advent 2011.

Every shift in the way we celebrate the liturgy in the course of our history has been accompanied by praise and outcry. This was no different with the most recent change. Some people are very much for it while others are very vocally opposed. This holds true for both laypeople and clerics alike, even high ranking ones. Some say the changes go too far, others that they don't go far enough. On and on it goes.

Our calling as members of the church is to trust in the Holy Spirit at work, albeit in a sinful church and through fallible people. The beauty of the Catholic Church is that there is room for those who delight in singing Gregorian chant as well as those who clap hands and beat on the drums. So rather than set up theological barriers and delineate liturgical camps, let us build bridges we can cross together.

Dear Johan,

I read in the newspaper that a politician was refused Communion during the funeral of his mother. I was shocked. I know a lot has been written and said about this, however, who should be allowed to go to Communion? And who has the right to stop people from receiving Communion?

Gentle Reader—

The Catholic Church has a very clear communion policy. Only Catholics who are in the state of grace, that is, who are without mortal sin, are invited to receive Communion. The decision as to one's state of grace before receiving Communion is ordinarily left up to each communicant. However, in the course of its history, the Catholic Church has withheld Communion from certain individuals or groups of people. Sometimes this was accompanied with great episcopal or papal fanfare. One of the best known excommunications is undoubtedly the one of King Henry VIII, which resulted in the establishment of the Church of England.

The loss of one's state of grace as well as the definition of mortal sin are very specific; yet, they also allow some room for interpretation. Wisely, most bishops have decreed that the time of Communion is not the time for a communion minister to discern a communicant's state of grace. And rather than using punitive measures or public threats, some have engaged in the often more fruitful exercise of conversation. Actions by self-appointed communion police rarely result in greater devotion to the Blessed Sacrament, nor do they contribute to a deepening of the spirituality of all involved.

When deciding on who is worthy to receive Communion and who is not, let's remember how Pope Francis reminded us that Holy Communion is not a kind of reward given to those who are perfect; rather, it is medicine administered in the hospital of the soul, which is the church at prayer. With the words we speak before Communion, "Lord I am not worthy . . . but only say the word / and my soul shall be healed," we acknowledge our unworthiness and our profound belief that Jesus will heal our brokenness and make us whole, no matter who we are or what we have done. As one wise bishop once wishfully told me, "If only we would all look a bit deeper into our own soul . . ."

Dear Johan,

I was offended by the fact that we prayed for people with AIDS at Mass today. Apparently it was World AIDS Day. What is that? A day to honor people with AIDS? Why should that be mentioned in church?

Gentle Reader—

Just recently I attended daily Eucharist in our parish. I like daily Eucharist for its simplicity, which may come as a surprise to those who know my proclivity for more elaborate liturgies. My peaceful state of mind was quickly dashed as I witnessed the battle of prayers that ensued when the priest opened the intercessions for individual intentions. After the customary yet baffling series of "special intentions," we were subjected to several prayers that resembled political statements more so than prayers. Moreover, they seemed to be occasioned by one another and intended to cancel out the preceding intercession. I will refrain from giving an example but I suspect you have experienced what I am talking about.

I wonder if your somewhat polemical question was occasioned by such a prayer that you thought political and deemed inappropriate because it was related to AIDS. I hope and pray you resisted the temptation to offer a counter-prayer.

Surely, you loved Pope John Paul II. Did you know that on his apostolic visits throughout the world he made a point of stopping by hospices for HIV-AIDS patients? And did you know that he not only prayed *for* people with AIDS but also prayed *with* them?

At his midday *Angelus* address on November 30, 2003, the day before World AIDS Day, John Paul II said the following: "I pray for those struck by this plague, and I encourage all those in the Church who provide a priceless service of welcome, care, and spiritual accompaniment to these brothers and sisters of ours."

These are the words of a true Christian. These are the words of a saint. These are the words of Christ. Let's follow Pope John Paul and now Pope Francis as they show us how to be Christ to the world and live out the call for radical hospitality for all, free of all judgment and condescension.

Dear Johan,

Growing up I was told that it was a sin not to attend Mass on Sunday. And what about holy days of obligation? Do we still believe in all this?

Gentle Reader—

Let me ask you this: When you love someone, do you see it as an *obligation* to spend time with him or her? Or, would the person who has been saved from drowning ever think it a burden to thank his or her savior?

Although yours is a fair question, it also bespeaks a legalistic and minimalist approach to the celebration of the mysteries of our faith, which is rather regrettable and supremely sad. Would that there were no need for an obligation, at least not the kind that is imposed on us by the church, today.

Our current understanding of Sunday and holy days of obligation is that it has been imposed on us by the church, and rightfully so. By contrast, the early church had no such law because there simply was no need for it. The sense of "obligation" early Christians felt to celebrate Sunday Eucharist flowed from a deep personal and communal desire. Theirs was an inner obligation to the celebration of the Eucharist. They were so moved by the mystery of God's love for us that they simply could not but celebrate. Saint John Paul II in his apostolic letter *Dies Domini*, On Keeping the Lord's Day Holy, from 1998 calls it the "obligation of conscience."

As this "obligation of conscience" or inner desire started to wane, individual bishops found it necessary to remind the faithful that the Sunday assembly was not simply an option but rather a sacred duty. This kind of language can be found in local church documents dating back to the fourth century. Though the number and intensity of these documents increases over the centuries, it was not until 1917 when the Code of Canon Law defined the obligation to celebrate Eucharist on Sundays and holy days of obligation as universal law. This law was upheld by the 1983 Code of Canon Law. And the current *Catechism of the Catholic Church* identifies the deliberate failure to follow this obligation as a grave sin.

So, yes, we still abide by Sunday and holy day obligations. Both your question and my answer make me sad, though. On the one hand, I am saddened that we have punishing legislation in an attempt to encourage people to celebrate Sunday Eucharist. On the other hand, I am saddened by the fact that we have lost this sense of inner obligation. We might be better off if we were less legalistic and more spiritual when it comes to the celebration of the Eucharist. But maybe that is merely a liturgical reverie or fantasy?

Dear Johan,

When I called my parish to request the last rites for my mom, I was told we now call it the sacrament of the sick. And I should not have waited this long to request it. Can you help me understand?

Gentle Reader—

I hope they were nice about it. And indeed, there is a big difference between the two.

Before the Second Vatican Council, sacramental care of the sick was mostly limited to the very last moments of life. With much ceremony a priest visited a person at the end of his or her life. The priest first heard the dying person's confession. Following that he anointed the person with the oil of the sick. This was known as extreme unction. Finally, he would offer the dying person his or her last Communion or Viaticum. This Latin word implies that this would be the person's nourishment when making the journey from this life to the next. Because all of this happened at the end of a person's life, the combination of these three sacraments was known as the last rites. By the way, it was not unusual for a newly married couple to receive a last rites kit in the form of a cross as a wedding gift.

In light of the Second Vatican Council all the sacraments and liturgical celebrations were studied very carefully as to their theological meaning and historical accuracy. A major shift took place with regard to the last rites. Before the council, the sacrament was clearly seen as a passage rite accompanying the movement from this life to the next. Since then, the sacrament has been renamed to sacrament of the sick and is ranked with the sacrament of reconciliation as one of the sacraments of healing.

In the case of the sacrament of the sick, the notion of healing does not only refer to a bodily recovery, though that is clearly prayed for. Rather it implies a strengthening of the entire person (body, soul, and mind) in order to live fully within the limitations of the situation. The person may not be physically healed, but may be given the grace to embrace the illness and live as fully as possible.

When it comes to pastoral and sacramental care for those who are sick, we now have a much more inclusive approach. A person does not have to be on his or her deathbed to receive the sacrament. In addition, care has been broadened beyond the celebration of the sacrament and beyond the presence of ordained ministers.

I hope a priest was able to visit with you and your mom and celebrate the sacrament of the sick. I also hope your mom recovered from her illness. In the future, should she fall ill again, please don't hesitate to contact your parish not only so your mom may receive the sacrament but also so the parish may assist her and you during this difficult journey.

Dear Johan,

My mom requested to be cremated. I was surprised. She is very Catholic. And though I know the Catholic Church allows for cremation, I am not entirely comfortable with it. Any advice?

Gentle Reader–

Though explicit legislation forbidding cremation is relatively new, it has been the ancient custom for Catholics not to be cremated. Early Christians followed the Jewish custom of burying the bodies of the deceased. Jesus himself was laid in a tomb. And even when Christianity spread through the Roman Empire, where cremation was quite common, they retained the custom of burying their dead. Cremation more or less disappeared together with the Roman Empire, except maybe at times of overwhelming death by disease such as during epidemics of the plague.

Around the turn of the twentieth century cremation started to be practiced again in Europe. The Catholic Church interpreted this as a denial of the resurrection and ruled against the practice in the 1917 Code of Canon Law, even forbidding a funeral Mass for those who had been cremated. In 1963 this ban was lifted and the new Code of Canon Law of 1983 was adapted accordingly. In a 1997 appendix to the Order of Christian Funerals, the Congregation for Divine Worship approved cremation as an acceptable practice for Catholics.

However, though cremation is now permitted in the Catholic Church, there are a couple conditions. One, the preference is to have the body present for the funeral and that cremation takes place following the service. Nevertheless, the rite also makes provision for the possibility of cremation before the funeral service. In this case the cremated remains should be present at the funeral liturgy.

Two, the cremated remains are to be treated in the same way as the body would be treated. This means that the cremated remains should be buried properly. This precludes the scattering of remains in oceans and over mountaintops. It also precludes the keeping of cremated remains on one's mantle or in one's dresser.

As long as you observe the above you can feel completely comfortable fulfilling your mom's wishes.

Liturgical Vesture

Dear Johan,

I can't believe what people are wearing to church these days. Can't you do something about that?

Gentle Reader—

Believe me, I have tried, but people just don't like to be told what to wear. That will, however, not keep me from opining on the matter.

Shortly before I moved to the United States I was invited to join a group of other soon-to-be expats for an evening at the Belgian-American Foundation. The goal of the evening was to facilitate the transition from life in Europe to life in the United States. In addition to teaching us how to shop we were told what to wear. One of the points the American instructor made was that Europeans are much more formal than Americans. So, we were advised not to bring too many suits and formal outfits. Over the past 25 years, I have realized, however, that even if the majority of Americans are less formal than Europeans, there are different levels of informality. People tend to wear specific clothes to different events. Baseball games, picnics, fine dinners, and Sunday Eucharist require their own sets of clothes. Recently I have noticed, though, that some people come to church wearing Viking purple or Packer green. I suppose I should take consolation in the absence of the fake Viking hair and hats.

The reason for wearing certain clothes for certain occasions, be they formal or informal, is that clothes not only cover the body but they also communicate a message, whether intended or not.

Most important they communicate how the wearer feels about the event that takes place.

And of course, you are correct: there is indeed appropriate and inappropriate dress for worship, especially for liturgical ministers. Last week one of our servers wore tennis shoes that light up at every step. These were inappropriate for two reasons. First, tennis shoes should be worn for tennis and not for church. Second, they were distracting to the assembly. Rather than gazing at the cross the server was carrying, parishioners stared at his fancy footwear.

I know that the last thing people want me to say is that their outfit is inappropriate for church. So I won't. But just so you know, when I get up on Sunday morning and decide what to wear, I always ask myself if my attire is fitting for the celebration of the Eucharist, rather than mindlessly throwing on shorts, a Grateful Dead T-shirt, and flip-flops.

Dear Johan,

I never understood the significance of priests' robes, their layers and colors. Could you please explain?

Gentle Reader—

The vestments worn by the liturgical ministers point to their function within the church. The alb, the white tunic, is the common vesture of all the baptized. The word alb comes from the Latin word *albus*, which means white.

Liturgical ministers wear albs to indicate that they minister by virtue of their baptism. Technically speaking, all the baptized could wear such a garment when attending the liturgy. In many churches the newly baptized (neophytes) wear albs during the

Easter Vigil. Some churches even invite the neophytes to wear their albs throughout the entire Easter season.

The stole is the long scarf-like garment worn by the deacon, the priest, and the bishop. The deacon wears the stole on the left shoulder, while the priest and the bishop wear it over both shoulders. Over the stole, priests and bishops wear a chasuble, the long garment worn for the celebration of the Eucharist. On occasion, they will wear a cope (sort of like a cape) for the beginning of a solemn Eucharist such as on Palm Sunday or for the celebration of the Liturgy of the Hours. In addition, typical liturgical garb for the bishop includes the crosier (staff), the miter (bishop's hat), and the pectoral cross.

The colors of the vestments relate to the liturgical season or feast. There are four basic colors: green for Ordinary Time; violet for Advent and Lent; white/gold for Christmas, Easter, and certain solemnities and feasts; red for Pentecost, Passion Sunday, Good Friday, and feasts of martyrs. In addition, rose may be used on the Third Sunday of Advent and Fourth Sunday of Lent while black may be used for funerals. The color blue, which is increasingly more popular for Advent, is not an official liturgical color. But then again, this is a detail only liturgists lose sleep over.

Footnote: To those of you who prefer the priest wear purple on days when the Vikings play, I say: advise them to play during Advent or Lent.

Dear Johan,

We have a set of extremely beautiful blue vestments for Advent. They are made of silk and are embroidered with silver and gold thread. Our new pastor will not wear them because they are the wrong color for Advent. Please tell me, is the color of Advent purple or blue?

Gentle Reader—

I am tempted to say that depends, but it really does not. The color for Advent is neither purple nor blue. The appropriate color is violet, except for the Third Sunday of Advent when the color is rose.

Over the course of the centuries the church has used different colors to indicate different seasons and feasts of the year and to mark different moments in the sacramental life of individual Christians. These colors are used to identify and assist the celebration. The current discipline of the Catholic Church pertaining to liturgical colors can be found in the Roman Missal, which is quite clear about which color is to be used for which feast.

- White is used during the seasons of Christmas and Easter as well as for the solemnities and feasts of Christ, Mary, and certain saints. White is also used for baptisms and weddings and may be used for funerals.
- Red is used on Palm Sunday, Good Friday, Pentecost, and the feasts of martyrs and certain other saints. Red may also be used for confirmation.
- Green is used during Ordinary Time.
- Violet is used during Advent and Lent and may be used for funerals.
- Rose is used on the Third Sunday of Advent (Gaudete Sunday) and on the Fourth Sunday of Lent (Laetare Sunday).
- Black may be used for funerals and the office of the dead.

However, though this is all made quite clear, the Roman Missal also indicates that more precious vestments may be used on more solemn and festive days even if these are not in the appropriate liturgical color. So, though your Advent vestments are blue, I see no reason why you should not be able to use them since they seem rather precious, and Advent, after all, is a solemn season.

Dear Johan,

What is the meaning of the little bonnet some clerics wear during Mass? And does the color mean something? I believe I have seen red and white versions.

Gentle Reader—

Your terminology is a bit lacking. So I am not sure what kind of ecclesiastical head wear you mean. I presume you are referring neither to the miter nor to the biretta but rather to the zucchetto. Nevertheless, just a few words about the two former before I discuss the latter.

The miter or mitre, from the Greek *mitra* for headband, is the pointed hat worn mostly by bishops during liturgical celebrations. The miter more than likely evolved from the headdress worn by officials of the Byzantine Empire.

A biretta is a square "bonnet" with three peaks and often with a tuft in the center that is worn by clerics during liturgical functions. The color of the biretta is reflective of the ecclesiastical rank of the person wearing it: red without tuft for cardinals, purple with purple tuft for bishops, and black with purple or black tuft for priests. Though not abolished, it is rare to see a priest wear a biretta these days. Bishops and cardinals are often seen wearing the biretta during liturgical events when they are not presiding and on other more ceremonial occasions.

The small, round skullcap worn by certain clerics is commonly referred to as the zucchetto. The official name is *pileolus*. *Pileolus* is the diminutive of *pileus*, which was the name of a cap worn by ancient Greeks and Romans. And just to satisfy your curiosity, some other names are *berettino* or small biretta, *subberitum* (meaning under the biretta), *submitrale* (meaning under the miter). The zucchetto is part of the liturgical vesture of certain ecclesiastical dignitaries and comes in different colors: white for the pope, red for cardinals, violet for bishops, and black for abbots and priests, though priests rarely wear a zucchetto. Franciscan friars may wear a brown zucchetto. During the celebration of the Eucharist, the zucchetto is removed from the preface till after Communion.

The origin of the zucchetto is somewhat unclear. It most likely does not predate the thirteenth century, when it starts to appear in paintings. Some suggest that it might be a smaller and less functional version of the older camauro, a skullcap that covered the ears and the back of the neck.

I know you did not ask about this, but since I made mention of it I feel like I need to expound on the camauro. It was intended to keep one's head warm during long services in cold and drafty churches. If you are not familiar with the camauro, just look for a picture of Pope Emeritus Benedict XVI during winter. The camauro is made out of red velvet lined with white ermine. The color red dates back to the time when red was the papal color, instead of today's customary white. He also wore the matching red velvet mozetta.

The mozetta is the short cape covering the shoulders similar to the pellegrina. The difference between the two is both in use and in style. The pellegrina is white and worn directly over the white cassock. This comprises the ordinary dress or house dress of the pope. For more ceremonial occasions the pellegrina is replaced with the mozetta. While the pellegrina is open in the front, the mozetta is buttoned and has a small hood in the back. It is worn over the rochet rather than directly over the cassock. The summer mozetta is made out of red satin, while the winter mozetta is made out of red velvet lined with white ermine to match the winter camauro.

While the custom of wearing the red satin mozetta was continued, both the camauro and winter mozetta were retired during the process of papal simplifications in light of Vatican II. Pope Benedict XVI brought them back. He also brought back the Easter mozetta, which is worn only during the Easter octave. It is made out of white damask trimmed with white ermine. It appears that Pope Francis has done away with the mozetta, among other traditional garb, altogether.

Dear Johan,

I am glad Pope Francis did away with all the frilly clothes, but why did he keep the white robe he is always wearing?

Gentle Reader—

"You will know them by their clothing" comes to mind. The traditional cassock or long simple robe worn by clerics functions or functioned as their day-to-day garb. This was not only done as a nod to simplicity but it was also a way of identifying clerics as they are easily recognized by what they wear. Although all clerics wear a cassock, the color of the cassock itself or its piping indicates the rank. The color for priests is black, bishops wear purple, cardinals wear read, and the pope wears white.

Though the current color for papal garb is white, the older color was red. According to legend, Pope Pius V (1566–72), who was a Dominican, insisted on wearing the white Dominican habit, thus introducing white as the color of the papal cassock. Though this is a lovely legend, artistic renditions as well as ceremonial and spiritual writings confirm that popes wore a white robe and a red mantle centuries before Pius V became pope. Guillaume Durand (1230–96), bishop of Mende, France, known for his allegorical interpretations of the liturgy, confirmed that the pope wore a white garment covered with a red mantle. The white, according to Durand, symbolizes innocence while the red charity, compassion, and a willingness to give his life for the flock. Another interpretation is that the white symbolizes the spiritual nature of the Petrine ministry while the red symbolizes the pope's worldly power. The red mantle, known in Latin as the *cappa rubea* or red cape, is said to have evolved from the Roman *clamide purpurea*. This was a large ceremonial mantle purportedly given to the pope by Emperor Constantine I to symbolize the so-called Donation of Constantine by which the emperor transferred authority of Rome and the Western part of the empire to the bishop of Rome. Though the document itself is an eighth-century forgery, it has been used to give historical weight to the worldly power of the papacy.

Thus, traditionally when a new pope is elected the red mantle symbolizing his worldly power is placed over the white cassock symbolizing his spiritual power. When Pope Francis emerged onto the loggia of St. Peter's Basilica after his election, he was wearing the white cassock and the white cassock only.

Dear Johan,

I saw a Mass on television and the bishop was wearing gloves and colorful shoes. In addition a lot was going on I had never seen before. It was quite interesting.

Gentle Reader–

You must be a post–Vatican II Catholic who was watching a celebration of the extraordinary form of the Roman Rite.

If you indeed are a post–Vatican II Catholic, you more than likely only experienced the liturgy of Paul VI. This is the liturgy according to the reforms of the Second Vatican Council. By contrast to the so-called Tridentine Mass, the Mass of Paul VI is much less ritualistic. The language is no longer Latin but rather the vernacular. The priest no longer has his back to the people but rather faces the people. And the people are expected to fully, actively, and consciously participate rather than simply attend.

Some Catholics did not take to the Reformed liturgy and sought permission to continue the celebration of the so-called Tridentine Rite. By virtue of their age, elderly priests were easily granted that permission. Somewhat striking is that already in 1971 in response to a request signed by Catholic and non-Catholic Brits,

Pope Paul VI granted permission for the celebration of the Tridentine Mass in England and Wales when the local bishop deemed this opportune. Since one of the petitioners was Agatha Christie, this indult is irreverently known as the "Agatha Christie Indult."

Pope John Paul II extended the permission to use the Roman Missal of Pius V published by John XXIII to the whole church with the indult *Quattuor Abhinc Annos* in 1984 and broadened the permission even further with the *motu proprio Ecclesia Dei* in 1988.

Pope Emeritus Benedict XVI, in his apostolic letter *Summorum Pontificum* of 2007, presents the Roman Missal of Paul VI as the ordinary expression of the law of prayer in the Catholic Church, while the Roman Missal of Pius V in the edition of John XXIII of 1962 is the extraordinary expression of the law of prayer. Both rites are to be seen as enjoying equal status in the liturgical life of the church. Please note that in addition to these two rites a good number of other rites exist as well, for example, the ancient Ambrosian and Gallican Rites and the much more recent Congolese Rite, which is an adaptation of the Roman Rite for the churches in Africa.

Dear Johan,

I noticed what looked like oversized red hats hanging from the ceiling on the cathedral of St. Louis. Can you tell me what they are?

Gentle Reader—

I thought no one would ever ask. Those are indeed hats. They are called galeros, or cardinal hats, and they are threatened with extinction.

Galeros have been part of a cardinal's official attire since they were first given out by Pope Innocent IV in 1245. It is a low-top wide-brimmed hat made out of red velvet lined with watered silk and adorned with thirty red tassels, fifteen on each side, though the tassels have varied in number over the years. The galero was used during the creation of cardinals until it was abolished by decree of Pope Paul VI in 1969, together with some other clerical garb that was deemed "over-the-top." With the tassels rolled up or dangling, they were worn by cardinals attending non-eucharistic papal ceremonies.

The galero is also featured crowning the coat of arms of cardinals, even until today when the galero itself has been abolished. The galero replaces the customary heraldic crown or helmet in coats of arms, those being thought too militaristic for ecclesiastics.

Similar hats were worn and used for the coats of arms by lower-ranking clerics as well. They differed in color and the number of tassels, the rule being the lower the rank, the lower the number of tassels.

Now back to St. Louis. It was customary to suspend a galero over a deceased cardinal's tomb. It was left there until it disintegrated, symbolizing the passing nature of all worldly things. In dioceses where cardinals are not buried in the cathedral, their galeros are suspended from the cathedral ceiling. In addition to the cathedral in St. Louis, many other cathedrals in the United States follow the same custom.

Though they are no longer handed out by the pope and though they have been abolished, an occasional galero has been spotted on more recently created cardinals. Maybe the galero is about to make a comeback?

Liturgical Year

Dear Johan,

Advent is my favorite season of the year. I love the fact that we take time to prepare for the birthday of Jesus. Sadly, I don't know the meaning of the word Advent. Do you know what it means and where it comes from?

Gentle Reader—

The notion of the birthday of Jesus makes me a little uncomfortable. It reminds me of an unfortunate "children's Mass" with birthday cake and birthday song. Thankfully, there were no candles to be blown out. How many should there have been anyway?

Just to be clear, the season of Advent is the time of preparation leading up to the solemnity of Christmas in all its theological complexities. It is marked by the four Sundays of Advent.

The English word Advent comes from the Latin *Adventus Domini*, meaning the coming of the Lord. Most of us understand this to mean Jesus' presence with us at Christmas as we commemorate and celebrate his birth. The full meaning of *Adventus Domini*, however, embraces Jesus' birth two thousand years ago, his presence with us today, as well as his return at the end of time. Advent thus becomes a time of preparation not only for the celebration of Jesus' birth on Christmas. It also is a time when we become more aware of Jesus' presence in our lives today. And it is a time during which we prepare for his Second Coming at the end of time.

As a result, when we pray *Maranatha* or "Come, Lord Jesus," we not only pray for his presence in our midst at Christmas but we also pray for his presence among us today. And, most astoundingly, we even pray for his Second Coming, thus hastening the end of time.

As Christians we believe that when Christ returns he will in-
augurate the completion of the messianic times. At that time, according to the prophet Isaiah, "They shall beat their swords into
plowshares / and their spears into pruning hooks" and "the wolf
shall be a guest of the lamb, / and the leopard shall lie down with
the kid." "There shall be no harm or ruin on all my holy moun-
tain." "The desert and the parched land . . . will bloom with
abundant flowers." Not surprisingly, these are lines taken from
readings used during the Advent season.

The beautiful season of Advent invites us to dream of that
perfect world without disasters, disease, or death; a world where
all God's children and all of creation exist together in perfect
harmony. It is also a season during which we commit ourselves
to making this harmonious world a bit more possible.

So, when we sing *Maranatha* let's do it with full voice and
heart and let's act in ways that will hasten the arrival of that perfect world.

I hope I did not ruin Advent for you.

Dear Johan,

I was struck by the priest wishing people a happy New Year on the
First Sunday of Advent. It made me wonder about the liturgical
calendar and how it connects to the civic calendar. Wouldn't it be
easier to have just one calendar? I find it confusing.

Gentle Reader—

I cannot help but ask, did he also inquire about your New Year's
resolutions?

But seriously, unlike space, which can easily be measured, time is much more elusive. So, be assured, you are not the only one to be confused by time. Throughout the ages we have tried to mark time as best we can by developing calendars based on the movement of the sun or the moon or a combination of the two. These calendars have allowed us to better relate to the seasons of the year and also to mark important events, both civic and religious.

Today the most widely known and used calendar is the Gregorian calendar. It was instituted by Pope Gregory XIII in 1582 as a corrective to the Julian calendar, instituted by Julius Caesar in 45 BC. By 1582, the Julian calendar was eleven days behind the solar cycle. Thus, the spring equinox, for example, fell around March 10 rather than around March 21. In order to reconnect the calendar with the solar cycle the pope ordered that eleven days simply be skipped. This happened in October 1582 when the calendar shifted from Thursday, October 4, 1582, the last day of the Julian calendar, to Friday, October 15, 1582, the first day of the Gregorian calendar. He also adjusted the calculation of leap years to avoid accumulating discrepancies between the calendar and the cycles of the sun.

Though some churches still use the Julian calendar, the Catholic Church and many other denominations base the computation of the liturgical year on the Gregorian calendar. As a result, Christmas in the liturgical calendar coincides with December 25 of the Gregorian calendar. This feast is one of many feasts that are connected to a specific date. There are also moveable feasts that are not connected with a specific date. Easter and all feasts and seasons connected to Easter, for example, change from year to year relative to the first full moon following the spring equinox (March 21). This formula to calculate the date of Easter was established by the First Council of Nicea (325). According to this council Easter is to be celebrated on the first Sunday following the first full moon, following the spring equinox. The council set March 21 as the spring equinox, though astrologically speaking March 20 is more often the actual date of the spring equinox.

The liturgical year, then, uses the Gregorian calendar yet exists in its own right. While the Gregorian calendar is tied to the cycles of the sun, the liturgical calendar is connected to the mystery of salvation. Thus the liturgical year as we know it today begins with the incarnation cycle (Advent and Christmas), which celebrates the birth of our salvation in Jesus Christ. Advent begins four Sundays before Christmas each year. Therefore the dates for the Sundays of Advent differ from year to year.

The other major season in the liturgical year, of course, is the paschal cycle (Lent and Easter), when we remember the life, death, and resurrection of Jesus. Together these two cycles comprise the most important moments of the liturgical year. The rest of the liturgical year unfolds around these two dates, concluding with the last Sunday of the year being Christ the King.

Given that we begin a new liturgical year on the First Sunday of Advent, it was appropriate for the priest to wish you a happy New Year. It would also have been appropriate to invite you to come up with some New Year's resolutions. After all, each new liturgical year we are given a new chance to do just a little better in terms of our Christian calling than the previous year.

Dear Johan,

Why do we celebrate Christmas on December 25? Is that really the day Jesus was born? I don't recall reading about it in the Scriptures.

Gentle Reader—

While December 25 is one of the most important celebrations of the year, it is good to remember that Christmas was not celebrated on December 25 until the fourth century. More important, it was not always very popular. Early Christian writers such as Origen (ca. 185–254) argued against celebrating the birth of Jesus, declaring birthday celebrations a pagan custom not to be imitated by Christians. Even in more recent times Christmas has been frowned upon. Puritans argued against the celebration of Christmas because of the lack of biblical references. This even led to the outlawing of Christmas by the General Court of Massachusetts Bay Colony between 1659 and 1681.

Though describing the circumstances of Jesus' birth, the Scriptures indeed do not give us any indication as to the actual date of his birth. As a result, when Christians were ready to start celebrating the birth of Jesus a date needed to be selected. Both January 6 and December 25 were contenders for the date. January 6 is the oldest date on which the incarnation was celebrated. Yet, in the end December 25 was adopted by most Christians.

There are two main theories for the selection of December 25 as the eventual date for Christmas: the *history hypothesis* and the *calculation hypothesis*.

The *calculation hypothesis* is based on the so-called whole-year theory, which holds that people of importance die on the same day they were born or conceived. Since some people believed that Jesus died on March 25; that would mean he was also conceived on March 25. Calculating nine months from March 25 lands his birth on December 25.

The *history hypothesis* posits that the celebration of the birth of Jesus was introduced on December 25 to supplant existing pagan festivities. In 274 Emperor Aurelian had restored the cult of *Sol Invictus*, the Invincible Sun. On December 25 the birth of the Invincible Sun was celebrated. This day was specifically chosen because it was the date of the winter solstice in the Julian calendar until it was moved to December 21 at the Council of Nicea in 325. Christians believed that Christ was the true Invincible Sun. The celebration of his birth thus happily coincides with the winter solstice.

In the end, I would not worry too much about the date of Christmas since it is nothing but a date. What is important, though, is what we celebrate on Christmas, namely, that God became one of us so we might become more like God. We can celebrate this on any date, really.

Dear Johan,

We tire of the Christmas tree in our home, but the children tell us we have to keep it up through the Baptism of the Lord. Is that true?

Gentle Reader—

Take consolation in the fact they did not request the tree to stay up through the feast of the Presentation of the Lord, which falls on February 2, forty days after Christmas. By some calculations this is the end of the Christmas season.

And yes, despite concerted efforts by the world of commerce to erase all signs of Christmas beginning on December 26, your children are correct. In the church and hopefully in your home the evergreens continue to stand and the poinsettias, though often visibly tired, persist.

The two main liturgical celebrations of the church, Christmas and Easter, have a time of preparation, respectively Advent and Lent, and a time of celebration, respectively Christmastide and Eastertide.

I suspect that the problem with Christmastide is that we do not really take Advent very seriously. As a matter of fact we often skip the season of Advent altogether and start celebrating Christmas on the First Sunday of Advent, if not before. It is difficult to take Advent seriously when all of society insists on setting up Christmas trees, playing Christmas songs, and doling out Christmas wishes as soon as the last leftover turkey sandwich has been consumed. As a result, people are understandably tired of Christmas by the time Christmas comes around.

The recovery of a true Christmas season thus presumes the recovery of a true Advent season. But I am afraid this is almost a lost cause. So please, listen to your children and stand up against the hostile takeover of Christmas by commerce. Leave up your tree throughout Christmastide. And next year, resist the temptation to buy your Christmas tree until Christmas, even if your children protest. Instead, decorate your home with a beautiful Advent wreath and introduce the lighting of the candles, one by one on the successive Sundays of Advent.

Dear Johan,

When did we start referring to Three Kings' Day as Epiphany? I prefer Three Kings' Day. It's easier and it tells us what it is.

Gentle Reader–

Three Kings' Day may be easier but that does not make it correct. Let me reverse the question. When did we start referring to Epiphany as Three Kings' Day?

Today the Christmas season is punctuated by a number of liturgical celebrations, in chronological succession:

- the feast of the Holy Family on the Sunday between Christmas and New Year's, unless January 1 falls on a Sunday when it is celebrated on December 30;
- the solemnity of the Mother of God on January 1;

- the solemnity of the Epiphany, though originally celebrated on January 6, now mostly observed on the Sunday between January 2 and 8;

- and the feast of the Baptism of the Lord celebrated on the Sunday after Epiphany, unless Epiphany falls on January 7 or 8 when the feast of the Baptism of the Lord is celebrated the next day.

The most ancient of all these is the solemnity of the Epiphany with written evidence dating back to the end of the second century. By contrast the earliest known reference to the celebration of Christmas on December 25 is no older than 354 AD.

The word epiphany is the English transliteration of the Greek *epiphaneia*, meaning appearance, revelation, and manifestation. The feast of the Epiphany is thus the feast of the revelation of Jesus as the Son of God. It was also known as the theophany, *theophaneia* in Greek, meaning the revelation or appearance of God.

The original feast of the Epiphany celebrated the four major epiphanic moments in the life of Jesus all bundled in one:

- The first epiphany is the announcement to the shepherds, which we now celebrate on Christmas.

- The second is the revelation of Jesus as God to the magi, which is currently celebrated on Epiphany in the churches of the West. Thus your title of Three Kings' Day for this feast.

- The third is the revelation of Jesus as God during his baptism, which is now celebrated on the feast of the Baptism of the Lord.

- The fourth major revelation is Jesus' first miracle during the wedding feast at Cana when he changed water into wine. Though not accorded its own feast, the reading recounting this event is now read on the Sunday after the Baptism of the Lord during Year C, thus in close proximity to the other three celebrations.

The main theological reason why these epiphanic moments are now spread out over several celebrations is due to the importance of each one of them in its own right. The goal of each celebration is twofold: first, we celebrate each epiphany so we come to know God better, and second, we celebrate each epiphany so we may in turn lead lives that reveal God to the world.

Oh, and by the way, there is absolutely no evidence that the magi or wise men were kings. They were more likely astrologers.

Dear Johan,

A new season of Lent is approaching. And Easter will be here before we know it. I want to do it well this time around. What should I know?

Gentle Reader—

Yours is an important, though rather broad, question. I will see what I can do in the allotted space.

The paschal cycle (Lent and Eastertide) is the heart of the liturgical year. Together with the incarnation cycle (Advent and Christmastide) it celebrates the two great mysteries of our faith: the incarnation or the mystery of God becoming human and the paschal mystery of the life, death, and resurrection of Jesus.

The paschal cycle comprises a time of preparation (Lent) and a time of celebration (Eastertide). The hinge between these two is the Sacred Triduum.

The word *lent* comes from the Old English *lencten*, meaning springtime. In Germanic languages, a derivation of this word is still used to refer to springtime. Its use for the preparation time leading up to Easter is somewhat peculiar. Other languages use much clearer nomenclature such as "The Forty Days" and "The Time of Fasting." These seem to offer a more apt description of this liturgical season.

Lent is characterized by two major theological movements and three Lenten disciplines. The first and foremost movement is toward baptism. The catechumens, known as the elect after the Rite of Elections celebrated on the First Sunday of Lent, are preparing for the sacraments of initiation. Their movement is toward the baptismal waters. The baptized participate in the second movement, which is toward reconciliation, as we prepare ourselves to celebrate the Easter mysteries worthily. The three great Lenten disciplines of prayer, fasting, and almsgiving assist us in our journey toward baptism or reconciliation.

Lent culminates in the Sacred Triduum, the sacred three days of Holy Thursday, Good Friday, Holy Saturday, and Easter Sunday. You will note that there actually are four days and not three. In order to reconcile the four days and the three you simply have to know that we calculate in liturgical time, that is, from sunset to sunset. Thus the Sacred Triduum begins with sunset on Holy Thursday and runs through sunset on Easter Sunday. On Holy Thursday we remember how Jesus commanded us to celebrate the Eucharist and to wash one another's feet. In other words, he told us to pray and to serve. On Good Friday we remember Jesus' death and venerate the cross. On Holy Saturday we wait in silence for the arrival of dusk when we engage in the most important liturgy of the entire year: the great Easter Vigil, when we celebrate the mystery of Christ's life, death, and resurrection and our incorporation into that mystery by virtue of our baptism.

The fifty days of Eastertide are a time of unending joy and continued celebration. This poses a bit of a challenge as we love to prepare for a feast, but we really don't know how to celebrate, let alone for fifty long days. That's why Lent is such a great success, and Easter at a great loss. So maybe, if you really want the paschal cycle to be the best ever, you might want to concentrate on celebrating Easter for fifty days rather than one day or maybe two.

Two feasts punctuate Eastertide: Ascension and Pentecost. On Ascension Thursday, which is traditionally celebrated forty days after Easter, we remember the ascent of Christ into heaven. It is also the day when we celebrate that Christ promised the Holy Spirit to all his followers. The novena or nine days of prayer for the gifts of the Holy Spirit begins the next day. In the United States this feast is transferred to the Sunday after Ascension Thursday. Though this move makes it easier for everyone to observe the holy day, it does upset the liturgical order of things.

On Pentecost, which comes from the Greek for fiftieth day and is indeed celebrated fifty days after Easter, we celebrate the outpouring of the Holy Spirit on the apostles. From this day on, the apostles and their missionary successors have spread the message of Jesus to the world. Therefore, this feast also celebrates the birth of the church and its vital and diverse nature.

And here you have it in a nutshell: the paschal cycle described in 670 words. I hope you will find some of these words helpful as you prepare for a fruitful celebration of the paschal mystery.

Dear Johan,

Why is the anniversary of Jesus' torture and execution called "Good Friday"? Maybe the name lost something in translation from another language?

Gentle Reader—

From your question I surmise that you did not grow up with the Baltimore Catechism. Question 80 in said catechism answers your question very succinctly: "We call that day 'good' on which Christ died because by His death He showed His great love for man [*sic*], and purchased for him [*sic*] every blessing."

Still, I am not quite sure if you take issue with the name of the day itself or with the fact that the day is called good. So, to be sure, I will speak to both.

The naming of days has evolved over the years and differently so in different languages. Just looking at the days of the week in English they are all connected with pagan gods, though coming from different pantheons. Sunday, for example, is a translation of the Roman name for *Dies Solis* or Day of the Sun. Monday, or Day of the Moon, is a translation of the Roman *Dies Lunae*. Tuesday is dedicated to the Norse god Tiw. Wednesday is named after the Germanic god Wodan. Thursday is the day of Thor. Friday is the day of the Norse goddess Fríge. And Saturday takes us back to the Roman times as it is dedicated to Saturnus.

The Romance languages borrow directly from the Roman calendar and name the days after the moon (*lunes*, *lundi*) and the Roman gods Mars (*martes*, *mardi*), Mercury (*miércoles*, *mercredi*), Jupiter (*jueves*, *jeudi*), and Venus (*viernes*, *vendredi*). Saturday and Sunday are named borrowing from the liturgical calendar of the Catholic Church: *Dies Dominica* or Day of the Lord (*domingo*, *dimanche*) for Sunday and *Dies Sabati* or Sabbath (*sábado*, *samedi*).

Unlike other languages, the other days of the week in Latin according to the Catholic liturgical calendar are simply numbered. Thus Monday is simply known as *feria secunda* or second day since *Dies Dominica* is really the *feria prima* or first day. Friday is known as *feria sexta* or sixth day.

The official Latin name for Good Friday in the liturgical calendar is *Feria sexta in Passione Domini* or Day Six of our Lord's Passion.

Romance languages refer to this day as Holy Friday (*Viernes Santo*, *Vendredi Saint*). Germanic languages, on the other hand, refer to this day as Good Friday (Goede Vrijdag, *Kar Freitag*). The goodness of this day obviously does not refer to the sufferings of our Savior, but rather to the fact that through his suffering Jesus has conquered death and freed us from the lasting burden of sin. The name of the day embodies the paradox of the mystery itself, for it is by his suffering that we were saved. And it is through entering into his death that we live.

So, though other languages have other names that are clearly suitable, unless you decide to use *Feria sexta in Passione Domini*, Good Friday is a strong name too.

Dear Johan,

I noticed a service called *Tenebrae* creeping into the schedule for Holy Week in many parishes. I have never heard of such a service. Can you explain? Should I attend?

Gentle Reader—

It does not come as a surprise that you have not heard of Tenebrae since this service is not part of the principal liturgies of the Triduum. As you know, the main services of these three days consist of the celebration of the Lord's Supper on Holy Thursday, the celebration of the Lord's Passion on Good Friday, and the Easter Vigil on Holy Saturday. In addition, many churches celebrate morning prayer and midday prayer—skipping evening prayer in favor of the main service of the day, except for Good Friday. On that day, the main service is traditionally celebrated at 3:00 p.m. More and more churches have added an evening service that they call Tenebrae, which in essence is an adaptation of evening prayer.

During the Middle Ages a combined Matins and Lauds was celebrated at night during the Sacred Triduum. The name of these services was adopted from the incipit of the response to the reading for these services, which was *Tenebrae factae sunt*, freely translated as "darkness has fallen." The Tenebrae service on Good Friday was characterized by the gradual extinguishing of all lights, save one.

Since today there is no prescribed rite, different parishes have designed their own. Most of the time the service consists of a series of readings from Scriptures interspersed with the singing of psalms and hymns somewhat reminiscent of Christmas lessons and carols. During the service all candles and lights are extinguished until only one remains. This candle then is carried out of the church, symbolizing Christ's body being placed in the tomb and Jesus' descent into hell. At that point the community erupts in a sustained *strepitus* (Latin for loud noise) until the remaining candle is brought back into the church in anticipation of the celebration of the resurrection. The single candle is left burning as the assembly leaves the church, symbolizing Christ's ultimate triumph over death and darkness.

If you have never attended Tenebrae, I suggest you add this service to your liturgical schedule this year. You will not be disappointed.

Dear Johan,

Why are we celebrating Easter so late this year? Wouldn't it be easier if we celebrated Easter on the same day of the year like we do with Christmas?

Gentle Reader—

I suppose it would be easier and people would not have to ask, When is Easter this year? However, Easter by definition has to fall on a Sunday, the day of the resurrection. Therefore, it cannot be celebrated on a fixed date. But, please do not be embarrassed; throughout history learned theologians and saintly bishops alike have questioned the date of Easter.

As you note, certain feasts happen on fixed dates, for example, Christmas, which always falls on December 25. Other feasts are so-called moveable feasts that fall on different days of the calendar. The most important moveable feast is Easter. And because Easter moves, all feasts and seasons that are related to Easter move relative to the date of Easter. Ash Wednesday, which marks the beginning of Lent, and Pentecost, which marks the last day of the Easter season, are obviously dependent upon the date of Easter. However, Holy Trinity, which falls on the Sunday after Pentecost, and Corpus Christi, which falls on the Sunday after Holy Trinity, are dependent on the date of Easter as well. Even the solemnity of the Sacred Heart, which is celebrated on the Friday following Corpus Christi, and the feast of the Immaculate Heart of Mary, which is celebrated the day after the Sacred Heart of Jesus, are dependent upon the date of Easter.

It took a while to decide on the all-important date for Easter. Different bishops celebrated Easter on different dates based on different theologies. Some opted for the celebration of Easter on the fourteenth day or the day of the full moon of the month Nissan in the Jewish lunar calendar, as they believed it to be the day on which Jesus was crucified. Others desired to celebrate Easter on the following Sunday, the day of the Lord. Still others desired to disconnect the celebration of Easter from the Jewish calendar altogether. It was not until the First Council of Nicea (325) that the current formula for calculating the day of Easter was established. Since then Easter has been celebrated on the first Sunday after the first full moon following the spring equinox. The Council of Nicea also established that the date of the spring equinox was March 21, though meteorologically it often falls on March 20. Using this method, the earliest possible date for Easter can be March 22, which happened last in 1818 and will not happen again till 2285. The latest possible date for Easter is April 25, which happened last in 1943 and will not happen again until 2038.

And to complicate matters just one bit more, let me tell you about Orthodox Easter. The Orthodox churches follow the same computation system established by the First Council of Nicea.

However, because they still use the Julian calendar instead of the Gregorian calendar, we end up celebrating Easter on different dates. March 21 on the Julian calendar corresponds to April 3 on the Gregorian calendar. Thus Orthodox Easter falls between April 4 and May 8. By contrast, the Protestant churches follow the same system as the Catholic Church.

Dear Johan,

Was this a mistake or am I missing something? At Mass the priest mentioned we were celebrating the thirtieth Sunday of the year. According to my calendar, it was the forty-third. What's going on?

Gentle Reader—

An explanation is in order. After operating out of a liturgical calendar, as I have for most of my life, one sometimes forgets that other calendars exist. Or better, one lives in harmony with multiple calendars.

Though I am sure priests make mistakes, this was not one of them. However, he could maybe have been a bit more precise.

The priest was referring to one of the Sundays in Ordinary Time. These are the Sundays of the liturgical year that fall outside the incarnation cycle (Advent and Christmastide) and the paschal cycle (Lent and Eastertide). Had he used this terminology you might have noted that he was not speaking of just any numbered Sunday, but rather about the liturgical way of referring to Sunday.

As you know, the liturgical year begins on the First Sunday of Advent and ends with the solemnity of Christ the King, which is also known as the Thirty-Fourth Sunday in Ordinary Time. A liturgical year consists of thirty-three or thirty-four Sundays in Ordinary

Time depending on the year, four Sundays of Advent, three Sundays of Christmas, six Sundays of Lent, and eight Sundays of Easter.

Since you seem to be a person of numbers, you must have added all these up by now and noted that this makes for more Sundays than exist in one year. The reason for this is that certain Sundays are named twice. The third Sunday of the Christmas season, which is most often the feast of the Baptism of the Lord, also happens to be the first day of the first week of Ordinary Time. Thus the Sunday following the Baptism of the Lord is not the First Sunday in Ordinary Time, but the second. The same holds for Pentecost, which is also the first day of the following week of Ordinary Time. And to make matters even more complex, certain holy days take precedence over Ordinary Time Sundays such as Trinity Sunday and Corpus Christi, thus suppressing whichever Sunday they fall on. Those Sundays are silently counted as the first day of the next week in Ordinary Time.

I bet you wished you had never asked the question.

Dear Johan,

I understand what the seasons of Advent/Christmas and Lent/Easter mean. However, why do we refer to the rest of the liturgical year as Ordinary Time?

Gentle Reader—

You seem to suggest that you question the name of this season. If so, you are not alone. Many people are confused by the name.

The term "ordinary time" is a less than happy translation of the Latin *tempus ordinarium* since it seems to suggest that this time is common or unremarkable. A better translation would be "ordered time" or "measured time" or even "counted time." By contrast to the other liturgical seasons, the name of this season says nothing about the meaning or importance of the season. It merely indicates that during Ordinary Time we do not progress through one season into the next, but rather we move from one counted Sunday to another in an ordered fashion. From a theological point of view one could describe Ordinary Time as time ordered by Christian prayer for Christian living. It is the time during which we celebrate and live the great and salvific mystery of God's love for us as this was manifested in the life, death, and resurrection of Jesus Christ from one Sunday to the next.

If you are not interested in the minute details of the calculation of Ordinary Time, I advise you to stop here and move on.

Ordinary Time comprises mostly thirty-three and sometimes thirty-four weeks. A year has thirty-four Sundays when the dominical letter of the year is A or G. The dominical letter (from the Latin *dies dominica*) is the letter a Sunday has when marking the days with the letters A–G starting on January 1. For instance, in 2014, since January 1 (day A) fell on a Wednesday the first Sunday in January is January 5 (day E), which makes the dominical letter for 2014 the letter E. This means that all days carrying the letter E will be Sundays in 2014. In the year 2017 January 1 (day A) falls on a Sunday, thus the dominical letter is A. Therefore, 2017 will have thirty-four weeks in Ordinary Time rather than thirty-three. Leap years get two letters, one letter starting on 1-1 and another starting on 2-29. If there is an A or a G in this combination there will be thirty-four weeks in Ordinary Time that year.

Have I lost you yet?

There are two segments of Ordinary Time during the course of the year. Between the end of the Christmas season and the beginning of Lent we have four to nine weeks of Ordinary Time depending on when Lent begins. These weeks are counted forward so that the week following the last Sunday of the Christmas season is the first week of Ordinary Time. The last week of Ordinary Time in this winter segment is only a partial week because Ash Wednesday inaugurates Lent. The days following Ash Wednesday are known as Thursday, Friday, and Saturday after Ash Wednesday. The first week of Lent begins on the Sunday following Ash Wednesday.

The week after Pentecost inaugurates the second segment of Ordinary Time, which ends on Saturday before the First Sunday of Advent. This segment is numbered backward from the last Sunday in Ordinary Time, also known as Christ the King, which is always the Thirty-Fourth Sunday in Ordinary Time. As a result, the first segment of Ordinary Time may end with the fifth week in Ordinary Time while the second segment of Ordinary Time, which starts the day after Pentecost, may begin with the seventh week in Ordinary Time, thus skipping a week. Depending on the date of Easter and thus of Pentecost this second segment of Ordinary Time can comprise between twenty-four and twenty-eight Sundays.

Thus you can see, there is nothing ordinary about Ordinary Time, either in its content or in its calculation. If you made it to this point, you surely deserve a liturgical gold star.

Dear Johan,

When I was growing up we would always attend Mass on All Souls' Day. We were told to pray for our deceased family and friends. Is that still the case?

Gentle Reader—

It is. It is, though it may not appear to be so.

Our family and friends are extremely important to us. They have raised us. They have accompanied us on good days and bad days. They have made us who we are. All of us are linked to the great chain of life, which is both physical and spiritual.

This link has been very important in Catholic theology. Great artistic expressions of this may be found in one of the ancient churches in Ravenna as well as in the new cathedral in Los Angeles. In both places, the walls of the nave are covered with the images of saints who invite the worshipers into a procession through time and space. Every time we gather for liturgy we are not alone, but rather we gather with all our brothers and sisters in Christ, living and deceased. The mystical Body of Christ indeed is comprised of all the faithful, those who belong to our community, those who live far away and worship in a different language and liturgical style, and even those who have long since died and whose names have faded with time.

The church offers us the feasts of All Saints and All Souls to specifically remember those who have died. Some of them have joined the ranks of the saints; some of them have not yet reached that goal. Although death indeed may be seen as a great and dramatic transition from this life to the next, the journey to sainthood or perfect union with God continues, even after death.

Therefore, in the same way as we accompany our loved ones with our prayers during their lifetime, we also accompany them with our prayers once they have passed away. We do this in our daily prayers. We also do this every time we gather for the celebration of the Eucharist and most especially when the Eucharist is celebrated specifically for their intention. Finally, we do this on days set aside by the church for the celebration of the saints and the commemoration of all those who have gone before us. On All Saints' Day we give thanks for those who have attained sainthood and are our great examples in the faith. On All Souls' Day we pray for all those who after death continue their journey toward holiness.

The customs of celebrating the Eucharist, visiting cemeteries, and so on, that were popular for All Souls' Day appear to have mostly disappeared in the West. On the other hand, the Latino traditions surrounding the *Dia de los Muertos* with the construction of "altars of the dead" are strong and seem to bring new life to this important day in the liturgical life of the entire church. This may result in a rejuvenation of the venerable tradition of praying for our beloved dead in general, but more specifically on these important days of the liturgical year.

Dear Johan,

Although Halloween fell on a Sunday this year we did not celebrate it. What a missed opportunity. Why was that? I was disappointed.

Gentle Reader–

Simply put: we didn't because we shouldn't. And why are you not asking about All Saints' Day and All Souls' Day? They are actually legitimate. Let me therefore start with All Saints and All Souls. After that I will address your most worthy concern with the liturgical celebration of Halloween.

From the very beginning, the Catholic Church has honored the martyrs and saints. They were buried with respect. Their tombs were decorated and visited by the faithful. And they were especially honored on their *dies natalis*, the day of their birth into heaven.

Already in the fourth century there are indications that in addition to remembering saints on their *dies natalis*, there was also a day set aside to honor all the martyrs and saints. This may have resulted from the fact that there were not enough dates on the calendar to honor all the martyrs, especially after the most brutal persecution of Christians under Emperor Diocletian (284–305).

Different regions observed the feast of All Saints on different days, for example, the Friday after Easter, the Sunday after Pentecost, May 13, and November 1.

Two events that happened in Rome are of note in terms of the date of All Saints' Day. First, after receiving the Pantheon as a gift from the emperor, Pope Boniface IV (608–15) dedicated it to Mary and all the martyrs on May 13, 609 or 610. In preparation of this dedication Pope Boniface is said to have brought the relics of numerous early Christian martyrs from the catacombs to be buried in the Pantheon. This specific date may have been selected by the pope because it was already a date on which all the martyrs were honored or this dedication may have given further impetus for the celebration of all the martyrs on this date.

In 835 Pope Gregory IV (827–44) established the feast of All Saints on November 1. He thus solidified the intention of his predecessor Pope Gregory III (731–41) to move the celebration of All Saints to November 1, the day on which he dedicated a chapel in St. Peter's Basilica to all the saints buried both in Rome and throughout the world.

All Souls' Day, which is officially known as the Commemoration of All the Faithful Departed and in some countries also known as Day of the Dead, is rooted in the ancient custom of the Catholic Church to pray for the dead. Though the selection of November 2 as the universal date for said commemoration only dates back to the sixteenth century, there is evidence of earlier such celebrations on other dates going back to the seventh century. The connection of the celebration of All Saints and the commemoration of All Souls was very fortuitous as we remember all those who have gone before us back-to-back.

Obviously, Halloween is very much connected with the solemnity of All Saints and the feast of All Souls. The old name of All Saints was All Hallowmas. As is customary in the liturgical calendar, feasts really begin at sunset on the eve of the feast (e.g., Christmas Eve), as was and still is the Jewish custom. Thus All Hallows' Eve starts the celebration of All Hallowmas.

A number of things have happened. First, the name All Hallows' Eve has contracted into Halloween. Second, the Christian celebration was "amended" with rituals that have both pagan and commercial undertones. Borrowing from pre-Christian cosmology and supported by the wizardry of commerce, Halloween is about ghosts and ghouls overshadowing and contrasting with the saints and souls of the Catholic celebration. Though I don't mean to be the Grinch of Halloween, I would like to put it in context and plead for a greater emphasis on All Saints and All Souls. And I think the Day of the Dead celebrated by the Latino community may do just that.

By the way, when All Saints' Day falls on a Sunday its celebration supersedes the Sunday celebration. This also holds for All Souls' Day. By contrast, when October 31 falls on a Sunday we celebrate the liturgy prescribed for that Sunday simply because Halloween does not figure in the liturgical calendar of the Roman Catholic Church.

Dear Johan,

At Mass, people keep making references to Years A, B, and C. That all sounds like gibberish to me. What are they talking about? This must be another of those Catholic oddities.

Gentle Reader—

I know it sounds a bit crazy. Dare I add to the confusion by mentioning that we also have Years I and II? Do not fear, though, it will all make sense soon. And please relax, it is not just a Catholic thing.

The letters A, B, and C and the numbers I and II allow us to know what readings ought to be used during the Eucharist on any given day. The letters pertain to the Sunday readings indicating that there are three cycles of readings each covering an entire year. The numbers pertain to the weekday readings indicating that there are two cycles of weekday readings each covering an entire year. As a result, the Lectionary, which contains all the readings for the celebration of the Eucharist, comprises Years A, B, and C as well as Years I and II.

Let's delve just a little bit further into the history of the Lectionary as knowledge of history provides much needed perspective. Sometimes people seem to think that the Lectionary was given to us by Jesus himself. Though of course the Bible contains the word of God, it did not come with instructions as to what ought to be proclaimed when. That, we had to discover over the course of our liturgical history. And discover, we did.

Borrowing from their own Jewish tradition, early Christians continued the custom of reading Scripture when they gathered. At first they must have read from the so-called Old Testament books and shared their memories of Jesus. Toward the end of the first century there are indications that readings from the New Testament, that is, the letters of the apostles, were also included. And as soon as the gospels were written and circulated they were read as well. The way this was done is, however, not entirely clear and undoubtedly differed from region to region. *Lectio continua*, the continued reading of one book after another, may have been the practice in most early Christian churches.

By the fourth century the liturgical seasons were roughly established and the feasts of martyrs and saints started to fill out the liturgical year. The different seasons and feasts required their own specific readings. Thus the older custom of *lectio continua* was gradually abandoned in favor of prescribed readings matching each specific day.

At first these selections of readings were communicated through simple lists. Eventually the lists were replaced with veritable books. Thus there was the *Epistolarium* or Epistolary, which contained readings from the letters of the New Testament and select readings from the Old Testament, and the *Evangeliarium* or Evangeliary, which contained the gospel readings. The book that contained both is known as a *Lectionarium* or Lectionary, literally meaning book of lessons or readings. Though these lectionaries at first varied from region to region, by the thirteenth century the same Lectionary was used throughout most of the Catholic Church. This Lectionary recurred year after year, so there were no Years A, B, and C or I and II as of yet. This did not happen until the Second Vatican Council.

One of the goals of this council was to increase the emphasis on the word of God, both within and outside of the liturgy. Up until then only about 1 percent of the Old Testament and about 16.5 percent of the New Testament were read during the Eucharist. This changed dramatically as now we read about 13.5 percent of the Old Testament and 71.5 percent of the New Testament.

In order to accommodate this, the Lectionary was expanded from one recurring year to three recurring years (A, B, C) for Sunday and two recurring years (I, II) for weekdays. Each of these years begins with the new liturgical year on the first Sunday or weekday of Advent.

Sundays and solemnities have four readings. The first reading is taken from the Old Testament, except during Easter when it is taken from the New Testament. The second reading, which is best sung, is taken from the Psalms. The third reading is taken from the New Testament. The fourth reading is taken from one of the gospels. In terms of the gospels, Matthew is predominant in Year A, Mark in Year B, and Luke in Year C. The Gospel of St. John is used throughout each one of the years when appropriate, mostly during the Easter season.

Weekdays have three readings. The first reading is selected either from the Old Testament or the New Testament, relative to the season. The second reading is one of the Psalms. The third reading is taken from one of the gospels. These are read semi-continuously starting with Mark, followed by Matthew and Luke. John is read during the Easter season. The gospel readings are the same in Years I and II.

Finally, as to your suggestion that this might be an oddity specific to Catholics, it is not. Please note that after the Reformation several Protestant denominations continued to use the Roman Catholic Missal, albeit with some changes. When the Catholic Church adapted the post–Vatican II Sunday Lectionary, it was quickly adopted and adapted by different Protestant denominations. So, they too have Years A, B, and C. As a result, on many occasions the readings we use in our Catholic churches are also used in other Christian churches.

I probably tested your patience with this long answer but I hope you stuck with it and are now consoled by the fact that the naming of the Lectionary cycles is not just Catholic gibberish.